OUTSTANDING RESULTS!

Out of the Box Thinking for Business and Life

Anthology Compiled By:

JEAN OURSLER

DEDICATION

To all of those who crave Outstanding RESULTS!

TABLE OF CONTENTS

Introduction

Outstanding Results is the fifth book in the Results Anthology Series. The authors in this book will provide you out-of-the-box thinking you can use to achieve outstanding results in business and life.

Why do we keep publishing these books? The information in our Results books is changing people's lives. The authors in this book continue our mission of getting more business owners, entrepreneurs, corporate executives and employees, managers, financial planners, accountants, sales people, mothers, fathers, grandparents, aunts and uncles, the results they want so they can lead the lives they desire. The authors in this book are the cream of the crop in their chosen fields and provide a different way of thinking that can move you forward to achieve outstanding results.

When I decided to title this book Outstanding Results, I knew I was raising the bar. Outstanding results can mean many things but at the end of the day, achieving something that is outstanding takes a lot of time and hard work. Sometimes we don't want to put in the hard work it takes to achieve outstanding results. We don't know how to get there, or there are too many obstacles in our way.

If you are experiencing this or want to achieve outstanding results, then start reading. In fact, there are several ways to read this book. You can read it cover to cover learning the out-of-box techniques to achieve outstanding results. The other way is to pick and choose the chapters that most interest you and read just those. Either way, I know you will walk away with the advice and know-how you need to move your life and your business to a place of achieving outstanding results.

There is a lot of amazing, helpful information in this book. Therefore, I would suggest that you highlight, bend down pages, take notes with paper and pen, or on your device to keep track of all of your learnings. There will be many nuggets that you can use. I can guarantee that!

What is also great about this book is that it is here to support you in your life and your business so whether you read this book as a reference guide or as a motivational book or both, you will certainly learn what you need to achieve the breakthrough results you desire.

I know myself, and the authors of the Outstanding Results book welcome your thoughts and comments. Once you have read the book or a chapter, I would urge you to reach out to that specific author that really made you think or provided you with new information. Send an email to let them know your thoughts or provide some comments. I know all of us would appreciate your insights as to what moved you, changed you and got you to the results you deserve.

Thank you for letting us help you on your results oriented journey to greater success and an even more amazing life.

To Your RESULTS!

Jean

The Results Queen™

Chapter 1

Andy Murray and Ivan Lendl: How a Coach Makes a Difference

Authored by Jean Oursler

Who is Andy Murray? Who is Ivan Lendl? How do they relate to the topic of this chapter: How a Coach Makes a Difference? Why should you even care? For Andy Murray, if he hadn't hired Ivan Lendl as his coach, he would not have achieved the greatest result in his life. If a coach could help you achieve the greatest result in your life, would you hire one?

When people think about business coaching, they often question whether or not it will make any difference. Will it work for them?

Does it impact their performance? There are also people who think they can't afford it or it is a waste of time and money. They even may say, "I am not worth it or I will be judged because of it, or I can do it myself."

I didn't think much about coaching until I started my company. I always thought if you worked hard, then you would be rewarded. What could a coach do for me? I wasn't sure what I would get. I also thought they cost a lot of money. I didn't think I needed one. I was wrong.

When I started my company, I asked a friend who a year earlier had started a similar company to mine, "What would you have done differently?" Without hesitation, he stated "I would have hired a coach right away. I needed to focus on getting sales, and I needed help. I just couldn't do it by myself." He went on to explain about six months after realizing how much he needed help; he hired a coach, and it was the best decision he could have made because his sales increased. Here's the advice he gave me, "Don't wait to hire a coach. Hire one as soon as possible."

I started my business. I hired a coach.

I haven't looked back since.

I took his advice. In fact, I have had a coach from the first day I started my business and continue to have a coach to this day. I have worked with different coaches in different areas of my business. I have paid a lot of money for a coach, and I have paid practically nothing at all. Either way, I have always paid my coach first and myself second. There were times in my business I wasn't sure how I was going to afford my coach, but somehow I always had the ability to pay the invoice. I can say definitively I am more successful because I have a coach and I have the results to prove it.

Which brings me back to Andy Murray and Ivan Lendl. I read an article in the New York Times Magazine (de Jonge, 2012) that spoke about how the tennis player, Andy Murray decided to hire Ivan Lendl, one of the best tennis players of his time, to be his coach. I wasn't a tennis fan back then, but I was intrigued by the story. Why? It was about coaching, and I wanted to see how a coach could impact a person's performance.

The article explained how Murray wanted to become the number one tennis player in the world. However, for five years in a row, he was ranked No.4. Many thought Murray was a great tennis player. He just didn't have the results to show for it. Murray hired Lendl to change that.

The article went on to discuss that in a short period Murray began playing the best tennis of his life. The next major tennis event was at Wimbledon. I decided to watch to see if the coaching was working.

The results? Murray came in second at the 2012 Wimbledon Championships, the farthest he had ever gotten. A month later, he won the gold medal for men's single tennis. Two months later, he won The U.S. Open. The following year, he won the Wimbledon Championships. Based on the results, I would say the coaching was working.

Notice Andy achieved outstanding short-term results. He also achieved outstanding long-term results. However, how do you know that it was the coaching and not something else?

What I didn't mention, is Andy and Ivan parted ways in March 2014 (Briggs, 2014). There were many reasons. Andy had surgery. Their schedules weren't coinciding. Neither one was committing the time needed to be successful.

This happens in coaching relationships. You outgrow a coach. You get busy. You get successful. You fall out of love. Is it time to give up your coach? I say yes. Coaching has a lifecycle. You can coach with someone 30 days or 30 years. However, there may come a time when you need to find a new coach or even add another coach. The one thing I will stress is not to give up coaching. Why? It works.

What few people realize is coaching comes down to managing your mindset. When you are at the top of your game or want to be at the top of your game, I believe it is about managing your mindset, not your skill set.

Unfortunately, many people confuse the two. They often are looking to take the next training course or workshop, hoping to achieve outstanding results but it doesn't work. So what do they do? They keep attending more training courses and more workshops hoping for different results. If this is you, stop when you get to this point. You need a coach, not another course. I find only a coach can identify those areas that are holding you back. Not only do they identify them but they can minimize or even eliminate them to help you breakthrough to greater success.

How do I know this? I did say I have been working with a coach for some time. I also coach people to achieve the outstanding results they want but have not yet been able to achieve.

What I find with my coaching clients, is they don't see the small things holding them back. They may not have the courage to try something new. They need help strategizing with someone who knows it will work and will guide them through the obstacles. I know coaching works because I have experienced it from both sides – being a coach and receiving coaching.

So what happened to Andy in the time he was not in a coaching relationship with Ivan? Andy's performance was mixed. In 2014, he didn't win a single major title. In fact, he fell from No 4 to No. 6. In 2015, he did lead Great Britain to their first Davis Cup in 79 years, but again he did not win a single major title. However, he did go from No. 6 to No. 2 (ATP World Tour, n.d.).

I realize some people have hired a coach and have not achieved the results they wanted. Unfortunately, there are no regulations in the coaching industry. That means anyone can become a coach at any time. This is one of the reasons I have always offered a money back guarantee. I want to make sure people get the results they want.

However, achieving outstanding results can take time. When you are in a coaching relationship, it is important to set expectations and define the results you want to achieve. You want to know the person you are working with will assist you in achieving what you want.

Additionally, it takes two to be successful when you are working with a coach. That means you have to participate as well. I have been in coaching relationships where the person I am coaching continually says to me, "teach me." While I am happy to keep teaching, there is a point where my clients have to execute. There is no silver bullet to fix the challenges they face. It is hard work to overcome barriers. It is hard work to achieve outstanding results. Both the coach and client have to work together.

That is one of the reasons I think the Lendl-Murray coaching relationship fell apart. Neither one was willing to commit to the hard work (Briggs, 2014). However, in 2016, Murray and Lendl decided to resume their coaching relationship. Murray said, "The most successful period of my career was while I was working with Ivan. He's single-minded and knows what it takes to win the big events. I know what he can offer. The experiences he had psychologically helped me in the major competitions are obviously the events I'm trying to win and am competing for. I hope he can bring that same experience and those same benefits that he did last time" (Mitchell, 2016). At the end of the 2016 tennis season, Murray became the number one tennis player in the world with Ivan Lendl by his side.

Lendl is not there to teach Murray tennis. He is there to provide direction and to mentor. It is not about Murray's skill set. It is about Murray's mindset. Remember I said if Andy Murray hadn't hire Ivan Lendl as his coach, he would not have achieved the greatest result in his life? What can a coach do for you? Are you ready to hire a coach so you can achieve the greatest result of your life?

References

ATP World Tour. (n.d.). Andy Murray | Rankings Breakdown | ATP World Tour | Tennis. Retrieved December 20, 2016, from http://www.atpworldtour.com/en/players/andy-murray/mc10/rankings-breakdown

Briggs, S. (2014, March 19). Ivan Lendl and Andy Murray split as coach is unable to commit to the Scot's dates with destiny. Retrieved December 20, 2016, from http://www.telegraph.co.uk/sport/tennis/andymurray/10708657

/Ivan-Lendl-and-Andy-Murray-split-as-coach-is-unable-to-

commit-to-the-Scots-dates-with-destiny.html

de Jonge, P. (2012, June 24). Ivan Lendl Gets Back to Tennis. New

York Times Magazine, pp. 30-34.

Mitchell, K. (2016, June 12). Andy Murray welcomes back Ivan

Lendl as coach in time for Wimbledon. Retrieved December

20, 2016, fromhttps://www.theguardian.com/sport/2016/jun/

12/andy-murray-ivan-lendl-coach

About Jean Oursler

Her clients have crowned Jean Oursler the Results Queen because they say she is all about getting the results they want. Jean specializes in Getting Results with entrepreneurs, business owners, accountants, financial planners and lawyers who hate sales and marketing and want their business to grow and thrive.

Her clients make low six-figure new business development sales within the first 12 months or less doing it in a way that makes them feel comfortable.

Are you ready for Remarkable RESULTS!?

Contact Jean today!

Websites:

For financial services: http://www.practicemanagement.com

Email: jean@moreresultsnow.com

Chapter 2

Step Beyond Yourself

Authored by Alisa Cortez, PhD

By very definition, to achieve outstanding results means performing at a different and/or better level than previously or in comparison to other results. So, quite simply, to achieve outstanding results, we need to think and act differently than we did to get the results we did before. We can do that by intentionally stepping beyond ourselves.

I know from the performance, leadership development, culture change/creation, and organizational transformation work I do thinking differently requires strong self-examination to ascertain our thinking about possibilities and limitations of what we can accomplish. Often, we need a coach or someone to challenge our understanding and help us see how our thinking contributes to, or detracts from, achieving the results we want. Once we understand how we perceive the world around us, its opportunity, and our goals, we can then work to shift from old ways of thinking and living that limit us or don't serve our interests. We can then create wholly new approaches to thinking and crafting the future and results we want and step into a new way of being.

To get us started, here's my short list of some of the approaches we can take to step beyond ourselves and achieve the outstanding results we yearn for. As a preface, let me say that while I am happy with the life I have today and proud of the person I am, I'm also not even remotely close to where I want to be and what I expect to achieve. So, I too use this list to continue to govern myself and work toward achieving the outstanding results I want for my life.

1. **Embrace Opportunity**: Opportunity often knocks at inconvenient times. We get offered a promotion at work

when we're busy at home with kids who are involved in countless activities, or we may already have a demanding job. Opportunities rarely circle back a second time when things may be easier, so seeing them as the gift they are and embracing them are key to getting outstanding results in life. Consider that the person who is offered the opportunity will become more capable, competent, and transformed by having navigated it, only preparing them more fully for the next opportunity.   Thus, we need to find the time and organize other parts of our lives to make room for opportunity and continue to expand ourselves.

a.   **Personal Share**: When I was new to Dallas, and my daughter was just a toddler, I was asked to join a local community service organization called Lakewood Service League by a neighbor who thought it would be a good way to get to know people and get established in my new city. I joined, got involved, met some fun women who became friends and got connected to the community. Then, within a year or so, I was asked to chair one of their fundraisers called Walk Wag & Run. I was, of course, reticent to do it at first – it was, after all, a big job that would require leading/inspiring 35 members, organizing the whole affair, and being responsible for the dollars raised and the experience registered by the participants and community. My reward was discovering my creativity, sense of agency to bring things from concept form to reality, and how much I enjoyed exercising my leadership abilities. I was then asked to serve as president of the League a few years later, which I did and loved. A couple of years later, I was asked to serve as chairman of the board of 35 members of the White Rock YMCA at a time when we, as a board, were tasked to raise $14 million to build a new facility. This was a very demanding time but absent these experiences, I would not have gained leadership experience or folded these valuable learning lessons into my person.

b. **Personal Share**: Similarly, it was not at all on my radar or aspiration list to become a radio show host. But one day in late November 2014, I received a call from Voice America wondering if I'd like to host my own show. Having just finished my post-doctoral research investing meaning in work in relation to identity, I thought it might afford me a venue to share my research, interest in life story, and passion for helping people more meaningfully and productively connect with their work…and it has.

2. **Assume a Positive Response to Life's Disappointments, Challenges, and Crises**: This might be akin to "when life gives you lemons, make lemonade." Difficult things are going to happen to all of us, inevitably. How we choose or find a way to respond sets the course of our lives and says a lot about who we are, and indeed, who we can become. If we can look for the rainbow in the rain, there just may be a pot of gold waiting for us.

a. **Personal Share**: When I was 19-years-old and living in Portland, Oregon, I worked for a hopelessly vibrant, intelligent German-American commercial real estate developer as his administrative assistant. I loved

17

working for this man – he was fun, taught me a lot about the world of work, and I was having fun in the rest of my life while working there. One day on his way to leave for lunch, he swung the office door wide open, his business suit and briefcase trailing in the breeze behind him, and over his shoulder declared, "You have to get out of here – go get an education, see the world, and do something with your life. But before you go, hire your replacement!" The door slammed shut abruptly behind him, symbolically. I sat there at my desk the entire time he was gone, and wrung my hands, wondering just what had happened. When he gleefully returned from lunch, as if nothing had happened, I stopped him at the door as he entered and stammered, "Are, are y.. you firing me??" He answered, "Yes, absolutely! You can do and be so much more!" I was at first devastated. I did hire my replacement and shed some tears on the way out. But this man completely saved my life (first by giving me the job and getting me out of the small town I lived in) and then setting me on an entirely different course that has been far more enriching than anything I could see for myself. I just had to lean in and see it for the gift it was. We are still friends, more than 30 years later!

b. **<u>Personal Share</u>**: When my husband of 16 years told me in December 2015 he wanted a divorce, I could immediately envision a better future for myself and our daughter. Of course, all the change and transition were incredibly stressful, but I would not trade the amazing transformation that has occurred for me – physically (lost 15 pounds), emotionally, spiritually, socially, and professionally – for anything. And I could immediately see the better future for all of us the moment he uttered the words. That change ushered in a completely new and improved life. I have told him a few times how thankful I am he set us both free.

3. **<u>Be Bold/Adventuresome</u>**: This is similar to embracing opportunities but with a higher level of gusto. Being bold and adventuresome means both seeking new ways to challenge ourselves and also responding to crazy opportunities to afford us entirely different vistas, ways of

being and of course results. It takes courage and sometimes just plain "grit" with a small dose of "crazy."

1. **Personal Share**: At age 25 when I was halfway through my Bachelor's degree (I did not start college until age 24), the man I had only begun dating two months prior let me know his company was transferring him from Portland, Oregon, where we both lived, to Madrid, Spain. I extended my hand to shake his, and said, "You're gonna do great." He pushed my well-intentioned hand away and said, "I think you should come with me." I honestly had not considered that possibility but immediately thought, "Well, what's holding me back? I'm a college student without debt, no career to leave, why not?" So, after a total of four months of knowing this man, I embarked on a journey that totally changed the trajectory of my entire life. Quite along the lines that boss I told you about earlier had directed, I followed him to Madrid. There we lived for six months and traveled together all over Western Europe as he worked. I got to use and refine the French I'd already

learned in my two years of college and further develop my Spanish to live well in Spain. I enrolled in a distance program with the University of Iowa to continue my Bachelors. Those six months were followed by a tour of two years living in Rio de Janeiro, Brazil where I learned Portuguese well and traveled all over South America while finishing my Bachelor's degree and getting halfway through my Master's. The experience completely transformed the way I saw the world and my place in it. Whereas before, I saw other countries outside the US as interesting plots on a map, so different and inaccessible, I now was integrated with them and actively participating in and being enriched by their diverse cultures. My parents and many friends thought I was nuts. Could it not have turned out well? Most certainly. But as Goethe says, "boldness has magic."

About Dr. Alisa Cortez

Alisa (Alise) Cortez, PhD, is a conference and keynote speaker, event emcee, author, and radio show host who helps people more meaningfully and productively connect with their work. The work we do matters, not just to ourselves, but to the team, organization, community, and planet we want to connect with and matter to - so let's make it count! "Dr. C," as she is affectionately called, is known for her warmth and humor to enlighten, enliven, and engage her audiences. A seasoned talent scout, her radio show Working on Purpose features guests who encourage listeners to pursue their dreams and equip organizations to create environments that inspire engagement, high performance, and make them want to stay.

Contact Alisa Today!

Website: http://www.alisecortez.com

Facebook: https://www.facebook.com/alisecortezandassociates

LinkedIn: https://www.linkedin.com/in/alisecortez

Twitter: http://twitter.com/alisecortez

Chapter 3

Where Do Outstanding Results Come From?

Authored by Gayle M Taylor-Ford, LSCSW, LCAC

Outstanding Results come from NO QUIT! My goals may change, modify, or evolve, but I do not quit them. I really started at the bottom, it just so happens that my bottom was much lower than many others.

In 1993, I was homeless and using drugs in Florida. I got the help I needed to get clean and returned to my home state of Kansas where there was family supportive of my lifestyle changes. By 1995, I was a single mother with a one-year-old, pregnant again, working the drive-through window at Hardee's, on food stamps, section-8 housing, no child support, and I had a Medicaid card for health insurance. Through the assistance of a vocational rehabilitation program, I returned to college and finished my degree. I had decided to become a Substance Abuse Counselor and chose a degree in Social Work to fit my goals. In May 1998, I graduated with a Bachelor of Social Work then continued and graduated with a Master's of Social Work in December 1999. I had completed my undergraduate work at a Mental Health Center and my graduate work at a VA Hospital.

Over the next three-and-a-half years, I worked four different jobs, mostly in nursing homes and as a director of Social Services in a small rural hospital. What I learned was I do not like working for other people. I like helping people; I like working with people; I like being a part of a team, but I do not like working for others. The next two years I kept a part-time job, sometimes two or three part-time jobs at a time, but started working for myself as well. I was even selling Tupperware to make sure I could provide for my two children. This was when I came up with the concept of my company

Therapy Services. There was a need in the community I lived in for someone to provide Behavior Therapy, Cognitive Therapy, and Substance Abuse counseling as part of the Home and Community Based Services, Traumatic Brain Injury Waiver of Medicaid. There was an independent living company that had plenty of clients and no one to refer them to. I did my research and developed a program and began serving the clients.

A year later I was approached by another professional who was a Substance Abuse Counselor. He was moving out of state and wanted to know if I wanted to take over doing Substance Abuse Evaluations for the local court system. This fit right into what I was already doing from home. The services I was providing were in-home services, and these new services could be provided at the local courthouse.

About six months later I was at the local county fair and talking to one of the County Commissioners I knew, as I had rented an apartment from him a few years prior. I told him what I was doing, and he asked if I would be interested in opening an actual office to provide outpatient substance abuse treatment. He said there was a need in the community and drug tax money available for grants. He explained I could request consideration for this money by scheduling a time to speak at a County Commission meeting. I wrote a three-page proposal and was granted close to twenty-thousand dollars to get started. I opened the office where it is today December 1, 2005.

By the spring of 2006, I added non-emergency medical transportation with just one minivan as I was having difficulty getting transportation for clients that needed to attend specialist appointments 50-100 miles from where we lived. I have gradually grown the non-emergency transportation into the largest part of my company today with 15 vehicles on the road. As part of this, I have the only Bariatric Wheel Chair Lift Van in the entire state that is licensed to provide services for Medicaid clients.

As time went on my practice has changed and evolved to accommodate the needs of the local community. In 2007, I tried opening a second office 60 miles away. I closed it after 18 months with lessons learned. Each year my company continues to grow in ways I never imagined when I was sitting in that vocational rehabilitation counselor's office twenty years ago. In fact, all those years ago, I never imagined owning my own company. I just knew this was the direction I wanted to take with my life.

Because I did not have a business background, there have been many lessons I have had to learn along the way. I would say the most important lessons I have learned are:

1. Choose your staff wisely.

2. An experienced accountant to do payroll, taxes, and accounts payable is a must.

3. Follow the rules and do things right the first time so you don't have to go back and redo or fix them later. It is much less work to just get it done right the first time.

4. Integrity is everything. Being honest and keeping your word goes a long way −especially in a small community.

5. If you feel passionate about something, do not take no for an answer.

6. Stay relevant in your field or scope of practice. Join and participate in professional organizations. Read professional material regularly.

7. Networking is essential. Stay in contact with other professionals on a regular basis.

Yes, my advice appears to be rather simple. I believe in keeping it simple. Twenty-five years ago, when I was homeless and addicted to drugs, I knew there was much missing in my life. I knew there had to be more to life than what I had. I just believed it was all out of reach for someone like me. I did not believe it to be possible that I would be writing this today as the owner of a small business with more than 20 employees. I do believe you must have passion for what you are doing if you are going to grow it and be successful. The most important piece of advice and wisdom I should offer is that if you too are seeking to achieve OUTSTANDING RESULTS, then you must never give up and above all Believe in Yourself.

About Gayle M Taylor-Ford, LSCSW, LCAC

Gayle M Taylor-Ford, LSCSW, LCAC lives in Overland Park, Kansas. She lives there with her two dogs, two sons, and two step-children along with her husband whom she is a caregiver for as he has MS. Gayle owns and operates Therapy Services LLC in Burlington, Kansas where they provide outpatient substance abuse treatment, behavior therapy and cognitive therapy for individuals with traumatic brain injury, and have 15 vehicles on the road providing non-emergency medical transportation for Medicaid recipients. Gayle is a board member for the International Pain Foundation and an active volunteer and frequent speaker for The Brain Injury Association of Kansas and Greater Kansas City.

Contact Gayle Today!

Gayle M Taylor-Ford, LSCSW, LCAC
Phone: 785-221-7560
Email: gayle@therapyservicesonline.com
LinkedIn: http://Linkin.com/in/gayle-taylor-ford-1b72553

Therapy Services LLC
420 Kennedy St.,
Burlington, KS 66839
Phone: 620-364-2606
Website: http://therapyservicesonline.com
Facebook: http://Facebook.com/therapyservicesonline

International Pain Foundation
Website: http://www.InternationalPain.org
Email: info@internationalpain.org
Facebook: http://Facebook.com/iPainFoundation
Twitter: http://Twitter.com/PowerOfPain

Chapter 4

Transformation to Outstanding Results

Authored by Jacqueline Brathwaite-West

Life gets hectic, and things just happen sometimes! Sometimes we get to plan our journey and pray that it all works out with the results we work so hard to achieve and the vision we have seen in the imageries in our minds, day in and day out. As women, we try to do it all, and some of us never realize our dreams because we divert to being a mom, wife, teacher, chef, fixer and the like. We put ourselves on the back burner so others can achieve their dreams, vision, and results. Stop and think what your life would be like if you put yourself first, guilt free to achieve your dreams, vision, and results.

I have been there, and I am here to tell you after years of being there for others and not myself I had to make the much-needed sacrifice and be a little selfish to achieve my dreams, vision and OUTSTANDING RESULTS for my life. It wasn't easy; the guilt laid on me by others, and self-guilt played heavily on my mind, spirit, and soul. Constantly questioning myself, should I move forward with what I want to do or just wait, and wait and wait. Then I had an awakening or should I say, a moment when I realized I would be waiting for the rest of my life for the perfect time. (Is there ever a perfect time?) So, I took the necessary steps to achieve what I wanted to do.

I began working on my second career in interior design while working in the computer industry. After receiving my Bachelors' Degree in Computer Information Systems and working hard to climb the corporate ladder, I realized I no longer wanted to stay in that industry. I came full circle back to my love for design, determined to get OUTSTANDING RESULTS. It was not easy, but it was worth it. I worked my butt off to move my dream to reality. I went back to school to Parson's School of Design, The New School in New York City. Moving with a purpose and staying focus through the tough times brought intangible success and satisfaction to my life. I even had to take a couple of steps back and go off course when the recession hit, but I did what I had to, and never gave up on my dream. To achieve OUTSTANDING RESULTS, you must be willing to make the sacrifices that come with it.

Not everyone will see your vision or believe in your vision, simply because they are not you. You must be willing to move beyond what others think and feel, yes get some advice along the way, I certainly did, but make sure that whatever advice is given to you, it fits with your purpose and vision. Take what you need and throw out the rest because no person can see your vision like you see it. Remember if it is for you, nothing can stop you from getting it!

You will get support, and sometimes you will not, being strong enough to keep going without support is vital to your success. I had a great support of family and friends, but there were times when I had to put on my big girl panties and do me. Having a mother and father that instilled in me anything is possible if you put your mind to it, certainly contributed to my success. As you are all aware, there are people that will try to block you from you purpose, dreams and results. You may even start to believe what is spilling out of their mouth (it's only natural), but refocus and stay steadfast. I often prayed as I still do for guidance, wisdom, and strength. Do whatever you do when things get tough and even when things are great to keep you heading in the right direction towards your vision. There is nothing sweeter and more fulfilling than bringing your vision to fruition. It won't always happen as you planned, but you MUST get back on course because life happens and the most unexpected things will pop up during your journey. I know that whatever comes my way in life, was sent to teach me and prepare me for what is to come. The unexpected can strengthen you or weaken you; it's your choice to decide how you want to handle it. I chose to keep moving towards my vision.

My vision was to start an interior design business, and that's what I achieved. Being from the beautiful island of Barbados I was always attracted to colors, I have always been fascinated by colors. It's easy for me to put colors together, it's just in my DNA. So I understand how I was drawn to the field of interior design. Some form of color is always involved in developing a design project. I never worked for an interior design firm, so a lot of lessons I learned, I learned through trial and error, but I would never change it. Yes, I am sure it could have been a little easier, or it may not have been, I will never know. What I do know for sure is that no one else can live my life for me. Starting a business is not easy, but it is rewarding in so many ways. Meeting and working with wonderful clients who trust me and my talent brings me tremendous joy. Being a woman of color in the interior design business has its challenges. Some people have their preconceived doubts and trust issues but miss out on my talent and miss the fun of building a wonderful relationship with me.

I am the president of J. West Design Services, LLC. I absolutely love the way that sounds when spoken. Not because it fills my ego, because of all it means. It means taking over 20 years of experience, knowledge, and resources to give my clients OUTSTANDING RESULTS in commercial and residential interior design. Outstanding results comes when you can speak fluently about your work, when you have passion, when you think outside the box, when you connect with your client's wants and needs, when you push the envelope, when you see their vision for their space, and when you see their face upon completion of the installation. I have experiences which can't be taught in school from a book, this experience comes from knowledge and resources I have built over the years with artisans, manufacturers, architects, contractors, builders, movers, the list goes on and on. What I bring to the table with each and every project makes me proud and confident to be the head representative, the president of J. West Design Services, LLC.

Working to make sure a space is functional, safe and aesthetically beautiful is just a generalization of what I do as an interior designer. Meeting that prospective client for the first time, interviewing them as they interview me is critical to the success of any project. It's important we can work well together. Educating the client is another vital part of the success of a project and the relationship. If the client is unclear about the process, billing, timeframes and budget, there will be a problem. It is my job and responsibility to make sure my client understands how each piece of the puzzle fits together to make it a smooth process. And making sure I clearly understand the client is also very important. Creating the design and managing the project for my client takes the worry and stress off them. I manage contractors, plumbers, electricians, and the ordering process of materials, furniture, artwork, accessories, window treatments, flooring and more. I strive to make the entire interior design project stress free and enjoyable for each client.

Now do not think everything I do goes exactly as planned each and every time. Part of my responsibility as the president is handling any problems, conflicts, issues that may arise. It's not always pretty, but it's handled. The last thing I want is for my client to deal with those things. Being in charge means taking the good with the bad because anything that goes wrong falls on me. It doesn't matter if someone on my team messes up, my client looks to me to fix it, and it gets fixed. I remember one project installation where the tile setter assumed the grout was delivered to the site the day before, but it wasn't. My client expected the tile to be installed that day and I was not going to disappoint, if I could help it. I didn't think twice about what I needed to do. I headed to a tile store (not close by), picked up the grout and delivered it to the site. You may think that's not a big deal, but if you are the client and you are expecting something you have waited months for to be completed, you would want it handled. Things happen that I can't control at times, but what I can control and change, I make it happen because that produces OUTSTANDING RESULTS for my valued and respected clients. Nothing is too small for me to do to make them happy and satisfied.

In the future I have plans to have a television show, working on my own line of products and a couple of other business projects. So look out for more OUTSTANDING RESULTS and thinking outside the box from me.

About Jacqueline Brathwaite-West

A graduate of Parsons School of Design, The New School and president of J. West Design Services Jacqueline Brathwaite-West is often asked to contribute her expertise, knowledge, and experience of over 20 years to various publications and newspapers on entrepreneurship, residential and commercial interior design. She has been featured in Market Watch, dgi Wire, Design NJ, and The Star Ledger to name a few. She is an allied member of the American Society of Interior Designers.

As an accomplished leader Jacqueline is known for her upbeat, outgoing and positive personality which naturally connects her to clients, building long lasting relationships. She has mentored and inspired entrepreneurs, interior designers and believes in giving back by volunteering, motivating others to live their life to the fullest and accomplishing their goals.

Jacqueline has received awards for Best of Houzz, Arts and Community Service, Business Women of the Year, and Leadership.

Contact Jacqueline Today!

Website: http://www.jwestdesignservices.com

Email: jacqueline@jwestdesignservices.com

Facebook: https://www.facebook.com/pg/J-West-Design-Services-LLC-368915288378/about/?tab=page_info

Chapter 5

Power of Positive Thinking

Authored by Jo Hausman, MBA

Life hands us challenges we don't always want. But how we accept and deal with the changes is what makes us the people we are today. If we learn to look at challenges in a positive way instead of as a defeat, more doors will open for us.

Although this chapter is on positive thinking, it wasn't always that way for me. I want to take you back to a time where life was real tough and tell you how I gained the perspective to make my way back –going from grief to great.

In July 2010, I lost my husband to a lengthy illness. He had been sick for two-and-a-half years, and it took a toll on all of us. Thankfully I had started a virtual assistant business in 2005, so I was still working at home and was able to care for him while he was sick. My son Cody was a senior in high school and graduated in May 2010. That summer in June, Cody had to have major jaw surgery, then July hits with Jim's passing then Cody is off to college in August. It was the summer I dubbed as "the summer from hell." During the midst of everything going on that summer I kept saying "Bring it on, bring it on I can handle it." That was how I was dealing with the pain of loss and everything else going on. Doesn't sound too positive yet does it?

So much for the negative; now let's talk positive. Jim was my second husband, and he taught me a lot about love and second chances. When we met, I had been a single mom for nearly eight years. I had questioned the dating scene. But after meeting Jim on our first date, he was sweet, charming and had a genuine loving smile. I was hooked. He loved us unconditionally and when he proposed he did it by asking if he could be Cody's dad and my husband. How sweet is that? I had yearned for a man who would love my son as his own, and he did that. Jim had grown up in an alcoholic household, so he had to learn how to be positive. He taught me that every day when he woke up he said it was going to be an "awesome positive day." Although I thought I was a positive person before I wasn't as much as I thought. Thankfully I listened to him and learned a lot about it.

I then went to a seminar that also taught me how to remain positive throughout the day. I learned how to retrain my brain to think in a positive way. I learned that life could get us down, but it is through the hard times the good times will shine through. Somedays when being positive is just a mere word pure determination has to kick in. This is where your inner strength and core come from. The world is a wonderful place to be in and how we handle and conduct ourselves proves that.

I used to be able to complain with the best of them. I am still guilty of it but really try to watch it. I like to give everyone the benefit of the doubt. Once I fully soaked in what Jim and the seminar were teaching me about thinking positive, I started to fully embrace life in a different light. I started to think of life in a positive, loving way.

Once Cody went off to college and the whole ordeal was sinking in, it took every ounce of energy I had to be positive, but I did. Even when I was out at the store, I would put on a smile so others could be inspired and it would make me feel better. I wasn't a ball of fun at that time, but I knew I could muster a smile. A lot of people brought me sunshine, and now I wanted to return the favor. Once my grief was subsiding it was time for me to shine on others.

A quote I made up for myself when I was going through the grief was this:

'Take one day at a time; if that is too much then one hour at a time and if still too much then one minute at a time. Remember to celebrate the small victories and then work to achieve the next small goal.' Jo Hausman

Keep making small goals until they turn into bigger and bigger ones. One day you will be able to look back and see how far you have come.

Let's take a look at retraining the brain to think in a positive light. It can be hard to do but so worth it!

When you are in a negative situation instead of thinking in a negative way, start thinking of the positive things going on in your life. For example, you are standing in line at the grocery store and the person ahead of you is taking a long time. You are in a hurry; your child is crying, and everything seems to be going wrong. Stop, take a pause, take a deep breath and try to relax.

Then start to think these positive thoughts:

I woke up today

I am Blessed

I am Loved.

It is a gorgeous day outside.

My child is fed.

I have a job.

Whatever it is you can feel grateful for that is what you need to say to yourself. That is retraining your brain to think positive.

Instead of being a naysayer why not start being a yea-sayer. What a difference in three little letters. Did you see and feel the difference between the two words? Your eyes and cheeks will light up when saying yea-sayer (not sure it is a word but it sounds good!). Good feeling isn't it?

There are many times when I feel rushed, panicked, stressed, or I'm overthinking something. But when I do I realize it and then stop, pause, take a break from thinking and just relax, I will lower my shoulders, slow down my breathing and exhale and realize "this too shall pass."

I will focus on other people's needs instead of my own. Many people are going through their own personal struggles and sometimes we know nothing about it. We need to show kindness through a smile or hug wherever we go. These acts of kindness are free. People love to see others smile especially when you are kind and genuine about it.

Don't bring yourself or others down by going into self-pity and negative talk. Once you learn to think and talk positive, people will see you in the positive light. You will feel lighter and brighter. Your smile will be more radiant than it ever has been. And you will be happier and more content.

What does it hurt to smile at someone? What does it hurt to talk positive instead of negative? Nothing. It's actually freeing to your soul, your mind, and your spirit.

Another way to start thinking in a positive way is to start journaling. Do you feel out of control and don't feel you have accomplished much? Start writing down your feelings and how you are reacting to the situation. It is a freeing feeling to release it to the universe and then let it go.

I have a friend who lost her husband. She told me she didn't want to "feel" during the holiday season because it hurt too much. I informed her she needs to feel to heal. As hard as it is, we must go through the grief process to heal. If we don't heal ourselves, the future will keep resorting to our past. Release the past and move on to a greater future.

Write down your goals and dreams. Then make a plan to make them happen. Put down dates to achieve them. Give yourself credit for them and cherish the small successes along the way to achieving them.

Delayed gratification seems to be a thing of the past these days. But when you find you can hold off something until later you will want it and work toward it. And you will be more grateful for it. If you want to take a trip; start saving your money and put a date on when you will make it happen.

Free yourself of negative talk and negative self-perception. Once you do these things and start your path to a life of positive thinking, a whole new world opens its doors for you. Be kind and friendly to others. Give others the respect they deserve. Are we all perfect? Not at all. But by being kind and friendly, you can show the world the kind of person you are. You can show others the kind of person the world needs more of.

You are Perfect. You are Blessed. You are Loved. Now go and be Positive and Give others your radiant smile.

About Jo Hausman, MBA

Jo Hausman is a leadership expert, entrepreneur, motivational speaker, International live radio talk show host and an Amazon Best Selling author in 4 motivational and business categories. She loves to speak with and coach others to become the best that they can be!

She earned her Masters of Business with emphasis in Entrepreneurship in March 2014 from the University of Sioux Falls in Sioux Falls, SD. She has owned and operated her own virtual assistant business since Sept 2005 and has coached people to become virtual assistants. In 2014, she opened up 2 new businesses, is a real estate investor and city council alderwoman.

Her expertise lies in starting businesses and she is excited to help you too! Her excitement and passion for what she does will be apparent through her work and speaking.

She has appeared on numerous television, radio, blogs and podcasts around the world. She is a contributing blogger to HuffingtonPost.com and her international live radio show airs live every   Tuesday   mornings   8am   CST   on

VoiceAmericaEmpowerment.com

Contact Jo Today!

Website: http://www.johausman.com

Email: jo@johausman.com

Radio Show: https://www.voiceamerica.com/show/2578/go-for-it

(My radio show page)

Twitter: http://www.twitter.com/jojova

Facebook: https://www.facebook.com/groups/GoForItNow/

LinkedIn: http://www.linkedin.com/in/hausmanjo

Chapter 6

Outstanding Results from a Small Business Perspective

Authored by Laryssa Slaton

Part One:

How do I define success and outstanding results? What is my purpose? Have I lost my direction or focus? Have you ever asked yourself any of these questions, either personally or professionally?

If you are like me, many questions consistently flow through your mind. I did not always have the mindset I have today. I was reared believing, as a woman, education was not important. I, like many women, thought I would just get married and live happily ever after. This scenario would've been great in a perfect world. But, I found out very young, we do not live in a perfect world!

I married right out of high school, to a mentally and physically abusive man and by age 24, I had two beautiful daughters. After seven years struggling to make it out of a bad marriage, I turned right around and found myself married a second time to someone who mentally abused me. By that time, I had moved 1,900 miles away from home and everything I'd known. After my second husband's heart attack, life was never the same. We divorced, and my girls, and I started our journey alone. As a single parent for 12 years, we moved 13 times, forcing my girls to change schools multiple times. I had no education and struggled to provide for my daughters. Eventually, I put myself through college, while working 50-60 hour weeks and graduated with a double degree in business, with accounting and financial management.

My degree led me down multiple business and accounting career paths. I was fortunate enough to see businesses in numerous levels of accounting, business set up, and financing, from single-owned companies, all the way to large, publicly-traded corporations, in various industries. During this time, I saw many holes in small businesses, and the idea for my own company took shape.

When the economy began to crash in 2008, I began to juggle bills, even though we lived within our means with no financial support. Fear of not providing for my girls hit hard, and I had to do something. So, I took a giant leap of faith. I cashed out my options with the gold mining company I was working for at the time, moved 700 miles away to Las Vegas, NV, bought a house and started a business. In 2010, Vegas was still in economic turmoil which made the first two years quite challenging. But, it takes times like these to propel us into who we are to become.

Part Two:

To define success and achievement, we must first look to ourselves. What does success mean to each of us individually? Is it reaching a certain dollar amount or worth? Is it a feeling? In the end, how will we know we've reached it?

Living in modern times, we must survive with enough money to support not only our needs but also our technology-driven lifestyle of desires. Most of us have some form of debt, some from a very young age. Did we know what we wanted when we were pushed out into the world? Many of us didn't, and that's ok!

Many of us get pushed into jobs where we are miserable working and making money for someone else. Being a corporate employee means you are working to make money for the shareholders, not you! Your time and paycheck are controlled by someone else. And unfortunately, this time can never be recaptured and replaced.

Part Three:

Many of us have a desire to work for ourselves, hoping to gain more control of our lives, success, and happiness. We all deserve a chance, right? But, running your own business is not just an idea, a sum of money, or high hopes! Unfortunately, a lot of small business owners find themselves working longer hours for less pay, no benefits, and more stress!

Small businesses make up a large portion of our economy today. The numbers of new businesses are skyrocketing every year. The Index of Entrepreneurial Activity states entrepreneurial activity is at its highest point in 15 years. The Kaufman Foundation reports 565,000 new businesses start each year (that's 6.8 million/year). Over the last two decades, foreign trade dollars have climbed from billions to trillions and is seen in almost every industry.

So why should we care? We should care because many external factors ,for example foreign trade, can cause the vast majority of new and existing businesses to fail. You might think, "This doesn't affect me." But it does. There are both internal and external forces in our economic system that cause fluctuating business cycles, and these cycles create a roller coaster effect for any business. Not every issue will have a direct impact on your business, but, everything in our economic system has a cause and effect. All causes and effects can directly or indirectly affect your business, and as a business owner, you MUST think like one!

According to Inc. Magazine and the National Business Incubator Association, 80 percent of new businesses fail within the first five years. Dun & Bradstreet states, 91 percent of businesses fail within the first ten years. As stated by the U.S. Census, only 3.9 percent of businesses make it to one million dollars, and only .6 percent make it to five million dollars. These are staggering figures.

To understand how to beat the odds, we must understand what creates the pitfall. The main causes of business failures are a lack of capital, poor management, and lack of accounting.

Living in what I call the "rising of the machines," software and apps tell us we are instant accountants. So then why are so many businesses still failing?

Numbers are the language of business. Accounting figures lead to reporting. Reporting equals information, which furthers the company's success by enabling better decisions and management. If you don't understand a double-entry ledger system, how do you know your reports are correct? Information is only as good as the person entering it. There are internal factors a business has control over and trend in data. Without this information, you may not be prepared for unexpected surprises!

So, how do you tread the rough waters of business cycles? How do you handle growth and down times?

Build your team! Don't take on the world alone. A plethora of outsourcing avenues today makes finding the right help very cost effective! Teammates should consist of accountants, lawyers, agents or any other industry-specific member needed.

Managing a business means generating capital. Without cash, there is no business! Excellent marketing and marketing plans are essential in today's ever-changing global markets. Build an intangible brand with a competitive advantage. Recognize target genera's which have shifted from baby-boomers to the millennials. This may mean a knowledge upgrade, especially if you're not of the millennial age.

Handle your business, don't let it handle you. Make sure you're not cutting the wrong corners. Proper management means the business should run WITHOUT you. A business is more valuable if it can run itself, especially if you're going to sell it.

Part Four:

Without proper planning or direction, many business owners struggle with financial losses, stress, and broken relationships, and then try again and again. Perseverance and consistency can certainly lead to success, but learn from mistakes and calculate risks before jumping. Find your direction. In the end, how will you know when you've achieved your goals?

Get honest with yourself. Find not only "what" you want, but "why" you want it. Pinning this down will help you find direction and your purpose. Instead of asking, "What business will make me money?" Ask yourself what your passion is. What would you want to do, even if you weren't getting paid for it? Take note of your thoughts, actions, dreams, and what you enjoy talking about. Once you find patterns in your activities, run with it and find a way to capitalize on it.

Those that make millions a year can still lack health and happiness. True happiness is not a temporary fix. When you stop measuring your worth by the size of your bank account, you start focusing on things that are more important and the money will begin to flow. If you're not doing what you love, you have a problem. Conscious awareness is the key that unlocks wealth.

What drives you through tough times? Reason, purpose, and direction. You need a reason bigger than just "making money." Making money is temporary and leads to fleeting emotion. What inspires you so much you can access levels of energy to complete things you never thought you were capable of, or others wouldn't have the stamina for? That is your reason, purpose, and direction.

The day I looked back on my life to acknowledge I raised great kids through many hardships, successfully owning multiple businesses, and helping others succeed as well, was the greatest reward. The day I could fly home for my parents, in their time of need at a moment's notice, with only one phone call, I knew the significance of life's perspective, which defined my feeling of success and accomplishments.

Find true clarity of direction, in your life and financial goals. Find your purpose, find your motivation, your inspiration, and your passion, or find an excuse. It's your choice!

About Laryssa Slaton

Laryssa Slaton is named the small business guru of Las Vegas, NV. She supports small businesses and entrepreneurs, through accounting and small business management, all across the nation. It is her quest to bridge economic gaps and to assist ownership success. Her vast array of expertise was developed throughout 15 years of accounting and finance experiences. Proven methods allow her to start, grow, or drive a company forward with unique small business accounting perspectives and controller-for-hire designed services.

Understanding, numbers are the language of business, Laryssa takes pride through mentorship and customized services to assist in building solid business foundations, which can withstand the various business cycles. With many successful businesses of her own, it's her mission to develop businesses an owner can celebrate and benefit from, not only financially, but within their personal lives.

Invitations are welcome, from those serious about succeeding in the small business environment.

Contact Laryssa Today!

Advanced Business Concepts, Inc.

Website: http://www.AdvBizConcepts.com

Phone: (702) 930-6333 or Toll Free (855) 775-6852

Email: Info@advbizconcepts.com or
LaryssaSlaton@advbizconcepts.com

Facebook: https://www.facebook.com/AdvBizConcepts and
http://www.facebook.com/Laryssa.Slaton

Twitter: http://twitter.com/AdvBizConcepts

LinkedIn: http://linkedin.com/in/laryssa-slaton-holton-05179225

Chapter 7

What's Love Got to Do with It? Was Tina Turner Wrong?

Authored by Eric A. Merz CBC

A few years ago, my wife and I attended our youngest daughter's graduation ceremony celebrating her Masters in Social Work from Cal State East Bay. The keynote speaker, Dr. Terry Jones, told the graduates and audience that Tina Turner had it all wrong. He said, "Love was much more than a second-hand emotion as the song goes." He was trying to make the point that love had everything to do with how these graduates were going to impact the world. While it may seem obvious that someone going into a field that directly helps others must have a love for his or her fellow man, it got me thinking about my work and anyone's work for that matter. Isn't love the reason why human beings serve one another? I thought about all the applications to business. If people could refocus their efforts on the purpose of loving others, what kind of impact could that have? Let's break it down into different segments of life and business and particularly the interactions that occur between human beings in those processes.

Faith and Family

The basic unit of most societies is the family nucleus. At the heart of the family is love. In our culture and many others, that love is founded on a belief in a higher power or their understanding of God's love. "Agape," love in the Greek language, denotes a charitable, selfless and unconditional love. Agape is the type of love that God possesses for His people and that family members have for one another. Agape is different than the Greek word "Eros," which speaks of sexuality. It is because of agape love families go to work each day, play together, eat together, pray together and live together through good and bad times. As children grow older, they leave the nest to start their own families using the same principles. Actions do speak louder than words. A healthy family behaves appropriately with one another. If appropriate actions are not practiced, the family unit may break down. If the lack of appropriate action is not evident, is it a symptom or a cause for family dysfunction? Either way, a family is often dysfunctional if that feeling of love is absent. Love binds the unit.

The Employee

Employees are shown love through the actions of their employer. This type of love is demonstrated by respect, honesty, clarity, encouragement, support, and openness. If love is not felt, it is not usually returned. In other words, if people feel no love where they work, they are simply performing a transaction for their time and effort. Additionally, it takes increased effort to "fake" love-like actions to keep up the charade. Eventually, something will give. Some employees may get their love fix at work from their co-workers who encourage them, cry, laugh and endure with them. Trust me; employees are looking for love. Those who have contact with vendors or customers may find it there. The question is, will they have enough fire in their belly to adequately make their stakeholders feel the love? Some employees may find love is in the actual work they perform. If they do, they are uniquely blessed and will probably spread the love. What is your organization doing to ensure that employees are feeling the love? Assessments such as DISC and Values may help organizations begin a dialog about some of these motivational issues as well as improve communication. This type of investment in people demonstrates a personal interest in those you work with and may be used as the foundation for love.

Vendors

Some might question why we would be concerned about loving our vendors. Vendors need to be strategic partners. They bring important products and services to the organization that helps it fulfill its promises to its customers. Managing the supply chain and key services is critical. We love it when we hit a home run with our clients; most vendors have the same desire. If they don't, it might be time to consider a change. If we treat them like we want to be treated by our customers, aren't they more likely to go the extra mile when we really need them to step up at a critical time? I have witnessed companies that have pushed a vendor for a delivery of service or product only to find out it wasn't really a 911. They pushed because other service providers have had problems delivering on time. It is demoralizing as a provider to spend sweat, worry, and overtime only to find out it was not necessary. Know what your vendors are capable of and order accordingly. Love is planning and making orders in advance. It is not passing on your lack of planning to your vendor and then expecting him to solve your problems. Love is saying what you mean and meaning what you say. Love is not flexing your muscles to make others nervous unnecessarily.

Customers

Customers need the most love of all. After all, we are in business to help them solve their problems. We need to start the love affair by first understanding what our customers need and want. What is most important to them? Price? Service? Quality? How does their buying process work? Are there seasons when they need more? Do they make these decisions on an ongoing basis, seasonally or annually? It is our job to assist the buyer in this process. It is not about our sales process; it is about their buying process.

What about customers who are a real pain in the butt? Well, the answer is "it depends." If we have failed in any way, we must accept the consequences, if it is in the realm of "professionalism." What constitutes professionalism may vary by industry or markets. Usually, the high road of laying the love on them and immediately fixing the problem shows the customer you have enough love to continue the relationship. Never take a customer for granted. There is no bank account of love from previous encounters. It is more like the day has only so many daylight hours; once the hours have passed, they are gone. You can't use yesterday's daylight to accomplish something today. Likewise, the customer only cares about what you have done lately (today) or now.

If customers do not feel valued (loved), they will walk at the first opportunity. People buy from people they like. If they are not comfortable with the interaction, they are likely to go a different way. Some types of transactions take years of cultivating a relationship to build rapport and trust. Sales people can monitor body language and voice tones during the interactions to gauge the amount of engagement that is occurring.

In customer service situations where customers have bought but need assistance to enjoy their purchase, it is imperative the customer representative is empathetic first and act immediately upon known needs. This action is equivalent to giving love directly to the customer. If the customer service encounter fails to meet the expectations of the customer, it is highly unlikely any loyalty for the company or its products will develop. After all, most customers are not family members and have no "agape" ties to bring patience to the situation. This is also the reason people should not do business with relatives. That family love could cloud judgment or bring false expectations to both sides of the aisle.

Spread the Love

So, what does love have to do with it? I would say it has everything to do with life and business. The basic human need for love must be present for business to be sustainably successful. Think of ways you can bring love into your business. Do you love your business or job? If not, what can you do to make it more loveable? Or should you face facts and move on to something else. Perhaps, you don't love the job; you love the compensation and what it can provide for your loved ones. That's great if there is a clear understanding of how that fulfills your purpose. That way love comes to the job through the love of your family. If you don't love your customers, but you love the people you work with, think about those people when you are dealing with your customers and what is best for them. This thought process will bring love into the customer relationship. If you don't like the people you work with, but love your boss, perform with others in a way that is always pleasing to your boss. Rarely, does someone have a love for all stakeholders. Wouldn't it be wonderful to try to create that kind of culture? What possibilities could abound? Wouldn't it be inherently more satisfying if business worked so well that families, employees, vendors and customers feel blessed and loved by doing business together? Please spread the love!

About Eric A. Merz CBC

Eric Merz is known as "the get real with your dreams" coach. Eric can help you take your dream and create a new reality. Because his proprietary methodologies focus on planning, people and processes, he can take "business as usual" and help create exceptional results. Eric believes that within each person there is unlocked potential to be released for outstanding results.

If you are a business owner or entrepreneur, looking to achieve more, then look no further than Coach Eric Merz. His clients say "Coach Eric Merz has provided me with the tools that drive the engine of accomplishment, as well as the lessons that steer the vehicle of life fulfillment." "Our profitability has made it possible for me to realize my dreams. I owe you a million thanks!"

If you are not getting the results in your business and life that you would like, then contact Coach Merz to schedule a consultation. Your dreams can become your reality.

Contact Eric Today!

Website: http://coachmerz.com/

Email: info@coachmerz.com

Phone: 661-343-2373

Chapter 8

Content is Not Only King—it's the Key to Your Marketing Success!

Authored by Monique de Maio

Recently, my agency did an industry survey asking people we knew—specifically those responsible for marketing—to tell us what was of greatest concern for them in the upcoming year. The top three concerns were email marketing, website marketing, and content marketing, followed closely by thought leadership. They all have one thing in common: content!

What is content?

Content is the single most powerful cylinder of your marketing engine; it is the hard drive of your computer; it is the brain of your nervous system—I think you get the point here.

As marketing consultants, we hear various versions of the same theme: we cannot create content internally; we need outside help. This is music to our ears and money in our pockets, as that is what we do best. Having said that, it may not always be the case that people who think they need content created externally really do. Let's dissect what content really is, or can be for you, your brand, your company, and your marketing success.

Positioning

Content communicates the positioning of your company or brand. In order to define your own positioning, it often helps to articulate those of others. As examples:

Apple: simple, sleek, intuitive user experience.

Disney: family-friendly; methodically consistent in its presentation, orchestration, and execution. Amazon: convenient, ubiquitous, personalized.

BMW: luxury, performance, a driver's car (i.e. "the ultimate driving machine").

Positioning expresses your brand's essence, voice, personality, DNA, attributes—or whatever you prefer to call it. Everything you put in the "public domain" should have a consistent positioning.

Communications

Communications are all of the ways you present your brand to the outside world—website, blogs, Facebook pages, LinkedIn profiles, Twitter feeds, newsletters, advertising, etc. These are all powered by content. In every place your brand appears, you have to create content by which prospective customers can find you, and current customers will understand why they should continue to work with you.

Once customers have found you, you want them to have a consistent and predictable experience. You need to ensure that all of your communications align with the image and attributes you built your company and brand on—your positioning. Imagine getting an Apple product in a black box with flowers all over it with complicated installment instructions. You would be disappointed and confused, and maybe a little angry, as this does not match your expectations of an Apple product's appearance and function.

Unique Selling Proposition

In my experience, many people do not spend enough time developing their unique selling proposition (USP) in a way that can inform and serve as a foundation for their content strategy and its subsequent execution.

This is especially prevalent among technology and technology services industries in the B2B (business-to-business) space; many brands think that being better, faster, and/or cheaper provide reason enough for someone to want to buy from them over a competitor. In the technology industry, however, these are not differentiating factors, which are necessary for creating a unique selling proposition. Brands must express what makes them different and special. In the words of marketing guru Simon Sinek, they must ask themselves, "What is our why?" He asserts—and I agree—that people don't buy what you do, they buy why you do it! Content helps you tell that "why" story.

Perceived Obstacles of Content Marketing

Clients often come to us for content strategy, development or execution because they feel they cannot do it on their own. Their perceived obstacles—which are often articulated as complaints about their inability to do these things—revolve around three key themes:

1. "I am/we are NOT creative enough."

2. "I/we don't write well enough."

3. "I am/we are just not strategic enough."

This can often be overlaid with, "There just isn't enough time for us to develop this skill . . . Just do it for us." Having said that, I would like to dissect these three assumed constraints one at a time in a way that may alter the way you think about content marketing and how you might be able to develop it for yourself.

Not Creative

"Thank you so much, Monique, that's a great idea! We could have never come up with this on our own . . . We just aren't very creative." I assert that creativity is like strength training; you have to develop your creative muscle, and continue to use it—methodically and religiously—or it atrophies.

At a creative workshop I attended years ago, we did an exercise that consisted of walking quickly around the room and pointing to or picking up objects and purposefully calling them by an incorrect name. For instance, picking up your desk plant and calling it "cat," looking at your computer and calling it "vacuum cleaner," etc. Doing this consistently for about a minute, in rapid fire, apparently helps re-wire the brain; it allows it to accept new and unknown information and process it differently than if you had sat at your desk, as always, and declared, "Ok, I have to be creative now!"

If you want to develop your creative muscle, establish an ongoing practice of exercising the "other side of the brain." Simple things like setting aside a half hour per day to free thinking, meditating, journaling, story writing, will help you think without self-imposed boundaries. You will find that when you get around to thinking about what you could and should say about your company, your products, and your services, new thoughts will come rushing in. You might want to try this!

Not Good Writers

I recently met a woman who was a self-proclaimed "poor writer." That reality finally shifted for her, however, when her assistant told her that her writing was excellent, but she was just terrible at grammar. She had had no appreciation for her writing because her written work had always come back from previous managers or proofreaders with lots of red marks all over it. It wasn't the content that was the problem—it was the grammar and punctuation. Are you one of those people that may not be strong in spelling or grammar but your ideas are clever, well thought out and appreciated by those who read them? When you figure out what you aren't particularly good at, or don't enjoy, send your work out! I don't particularly like proofreading my own work, plus, I find I cannot really "see" my errors. So, I call my proofreader!

For others, they don't have trouble once the words are on paper, but getting to that point poses the problem; they don't know what to write about or how to write about something. Often, this "writer's block" is not due to a deficiency of skill but a lack of inspiration. Finding ways to boost creativity would help.

Sometimes, though, people lack inspiration because they view writing as painful or a chore. Try changing your perspective on writing. Instead of seeing it as drudgery and an obligation, look at it as an opportunity to express yourself and make a statement.

Why not get some professional guidance on how to change your frame of mind? Maybe you would enjoy going to a creative writing workshop or a continuing education class about something completely outside your day-to-day job or profession. This out-of-the-box thinking may be just what you need to unblock your writer's block!

Not Strategic

This is my personal favorite and one that seems to recur regularly in my line of work. My clients tell me there is neither time nor appreciation in their organizations for the strategic thinking they know would benefit their businesses. It is certainly difficult to be "strategic" when your daily email inbox has hundreds of emails; your day is full of back-to-back meetings, and your boss expects you to "get stuff done." That may sound familiar to you as well.

Because of this "lack of time," the execution of the tactics are often delegated to far more junior people who are not seasoned enough to understand the strategy behind creating the content in the first place—if that strategy exists and has been articulated. "Let's have the intern do our social media campaign; I don't want to bother with 'that stuff.'" Does this sound at all familiar to you? It does to me! If I had a thousand dollars for every time I heard a version of that, I would be rich! By doing this, people are effectively relegating how the market experiences their brand to someone who has little to no industry, work or practical life experience, simply because they can operate an app or a social media platform. YIKES!

Being strategic is so necessary—more so today than ever before. Communications, marketing, advertising whether traditional or digital and social media—whatever you choose to focus on—have all become more complex and demanding from a content perspective. It has never been more important to have a strategy to create the right messaging, to the right prospective customer, at the right time, in the right place.   It's like saying you want to drive to California from New York, but you don't have time to consult a map! Not smart, and probably not very effective either.

Like the map to get you to California, the strategic plan with your positioning, messaging, USP's and the appropriate content that comes from it—will get you to your intended destination.

Summary & Recommendations

Make sure you create a culture in your organization that not only appreciates and rewards "doing" but also "thinking." A few ideas to consider implementing:

Set aside several hours of your week away from meetings, phone, emails to review, to analyze and think. What has been working, what is not working? How are your website, blog, email, and social metrics and analytics performing? What topics are trending in your industry and which are getting no traction? Do these topics marry to the lines of business your company needs to promote? Are the "hot topics" in alignment with what your senior executives are calling out as the "hot products and services"? This can help you with ideation and development of possible content.

To unblock creativity limitations, call a few key customers. Listen to what they have to say about their experiences with your company. Ask them what they like, dislike and would like to see improved. You will be amazed at the responses and the rich and actionable information you will be able to gather. Plus, they will be thrilled to be asked their opinions! Who doesn't like to share their opinions and observations? Often, when we have called our clients' customers, they tell us point blank what they want. Sometimes these are creative ideas, and some are even rather simple to execute.

For strategic enhancements to your process, create quarterly business reviews (QBRs) where your senior level executives can gather and share the learning, metrics and results they are seeing from their efforts and the market. This allows you to adjust as you go and create the content you need to drive optimal business results.

The right content can optimize all of your sales enablement and business development efforts. Many think of marketing as a burdensome but necessary cost, but they must remember that it can also drive sales and profits while also transforming your business.

Try some of these tricks and tips and see what opens up for you. I know something will. I'd bet my career on it.

About Monique de Maio

Monique has been communicating for people since she came to the United States from France with her family at the age of 5. Monique was the family interpreter and advocate for many years. Today, Monique helps her clients find their voices, develop their stories, engage their customers, and grow their sales.

Her marketing consulting firm of almost 20 years, ondemandCMO is a go to resource for clients as large as Dell, Intel, IBM, Motorola, among many others--and as small as start-ups and growth companies. Their speciality is the development and implementation of content marketing, lead generation, and sales enablement.

If you want to turbocharge your sales and marketing efforts, contact Monique.

Contact Monique Today!

Website: http://www.ondemandcmo.com

Email: monique@ondemandcmo.com

Phone: 201-444-1597

Twitter: http://twitter.com/ondemandcmo

LinkedIn: https://linkedin.com/in/monique...

Chapter 9

When Opportunity Knocks, Step Through the Door

Authored by Shelley Hancock

It was a Tuesday evening at 6 pm in the early months of 1990 that I received the phone call that would change my life. It was a woman that owned a skin care center in town. She proceeded to tell me that she had the opportunity to become the manager of a resort opening up in another state and she needed someone to run her skin care business, and she wanted that someone to be me. I was speechless for a few moments. This was not a phone call I could have ever imagined receiving. The first thing that went through my mind was "why me"? Was it really me that she meant to call?

Let me give you a little background about myself back then. I had only been a licensed Esthetician for 18 months. When I graduated from esthetic school, I went straight to work in a dermatology office, so I had no experience in the spa atmosphere, and I had absolutely no business background. Not a single college class, no experience whatsoever. Still, this woman chose me to watch over her business. Years later I would understand she saw something in me I didn't know about myself yet.

She needed her answer the following morning because she was booked on a flight later that afternoon. This was a big decision to make, and I had only 14 hours to make it. I had some heavy thinking to do and needless to say I did not sleep a wink that night.

My mind raced back and forth between the position at the dermatology office I had secured with hard work or the opportunity to run a business. Safety or the unknown. Stay with the status quo or venture out to bigger possibilities.

After a long restless night, I decided this was an opportunity that doesn't just drop in one's lap easily, and I couldn't let fear keep me from jumping in with both feet. I decided I was up for the challenge, ready for the adventure. She and I met at her center the next morning for three hours to go over as much about the business as we could in just three hours. She showed me her bookkeeping program, client information, scheduling system and where everything was in the treatment rooms. Then she left, and I never saw her again.

The next morning when I arrived at the center, I realized the magnitude of what I had just taken on. Here I sat with absolutely no experience on how to run a business. The only thing I had going for me was plenty of passion. I was so excited about this new adventure. I felt like a kid the night before Christmas. I don't recall ever feeling any fear, just excitement and that was probably my saving grace.

It wouldn't be until many years later I learned about the Law of Attraction. How what you think about comes about. Where you put your thoughts and what words you use is where your life will go. Well, all I ever thought about and talked about back then was how awesome it was to have this opportunity and how excited I was to build a successful business. Failure never even enter my mind. All these years later, I truly believe this is why I grew a very successful business. It certainly wasn't from having experience because I barely knew how to be a good esthetician let alone a good business owner.

As I took over this skin care business, I realized why she wanted to leave. It was not a booming business. My first week there I had only three clients. Even being so very slow, I would arrive at the center every morning at 9 am whether I had a client or not. I wanted to be there just in case the phone rang. I wanted to be there just in case someone happened to drop by. I dusted, and I rearranged and made it feel like mine. It was my way of telling the universe I was open for business! I am going to be successful.

When I did have a client, and they would ask me how things were going, my answer was always "fabulous; I'm super busy, and I couldn't be happier." I would say this even if it was Thursday and they were my first client of the week. I always spoke, "as if." I never told it like it was. Only tell it like it is if you like it like it is. I wanted to be busier, so I spoke as if I was busier and guess what? Fairly quickly, I was busier!

Three months later I called the owner and asked if she was coming back. She wasn't. So, we began negotiating for me to purchase the business. Two weeks later I became a business owner. Had I let fear take over when I first received her call I wouldn't be where I am today in my career. This business grew to be extremely successful, and I sold it in 2005 to start a new adventure mentoring my fellow estheticians.

Even with little experience as an esthetician and no experience as a business owner, I used my extreme passion to make it through. We can always find people to help us with what we don't know, but the passion has to come from within, and that can't be purchased.

A personal decision that affected my business in a positive way came in November of 2013. My husband and I uprooted ourselves and moved from Northern California to Southern California. I can do my consulting business from anywhere, and we were ready for a change of scenery. We moved to a small town in Orange County. We knew no one. From the outside looking in, it probably looked as if we closed our eyes, put our finger on a map, and that's where we ended up. We've learned so much from this adventure. We only had each other as we began life in our new town, so it solidified our relationship even further. We had to put ourselves out there to meet new people and create this new life. It's been an incredible journey. I believe the opportunities that have come our way would not have been available to us had we stayed put in Northern California. Passion and excitement are the keywords again. We had no fear.

In March of 2015, another opportunity for an adventure dropped into my lap and once again I jumped. I received a phone message from a company that wanted to chat with me about being a radio show host. I deleted the message; I thought I was being punked!

A week later they called again and this time I picked up the phone. The first thing out of my mouth again was "why me?" I was speaking with the executive producer, and he told me they have a staff that combs the internet watching videos. When they come across someone with a personality that would draw people in, and this person seems to be able to speak about numerous things, then they contact that person. They saw my YouTube videos and contacted me.

Once again I was speechless. Another incredible opportunity I could never have imagined was about to drop into my lap. The executive producer proceeded to interview me and by the end of the call I was about to become a radio show host. The next week I started my training, and my first show was scheduled for eight weeks out. It was all very overwhelming, but that excitement and passion kicked in to help me through. It wasn't until the week before my first show a little fear reared its ugly head. What am I doing? A radio show host? Seriously Shelley? My executive producer talked me off the ledge, and the first show went smooth, sweaty palms and all. Within a couple of months, my weekly radio show became fun. The nerves settled down, and I really began to enjoy myself.

It's going on two years now, and I'm ranked number three on the health and wellness channel. I get emails every day thanking me for the information I share. Some extremely interesting people have come into my life because of the show. Had I not jumped at this opportunity, our paths would never have crossed.

I wanted to share these three experiences with you in hopes that you may do the same one day when you are faced with an opportunity that looks overwhelming. Instead of letting fear hold you back, jump in with both feet and see where life takes you. My guess is that it will be places you could never have imagined and your life will be more fulfilled because of it. Step out. Be bold. Ignite your passion.

About Shelley Hancock

Shelley Hancock, (a.k.a 'The Gadget Gal'), is one of the most trusted esthetic advisors of our time and Founder of Shelley Hancock Consulting, an organization dedicated to helping estheticians increase their profits. After owning a successful skin care center for 29 years, Hancock expanded her focus so she could provide a deeper level of service to fellow estheticians. Through hands-on training, workshops and private consultations, she has now connected 1000s of beauty business owners with esthetic equipment that attracts a higher level client and helps build a more successful practice. "Most retailers think the relationship ends with purchase," explains Hancock. "I view it as just the beginning".

When she's not teaching, training, coaching or working with clients, you will find her recording her radio program for Voice America.

Contact Shelley Today!

Website: http://www.ShelleyHancock.com

Email: contactme@shelleyhancock.com

Chapter 10

Honor Spirit Harness Success

Authored by Deborah Livingston, SNUi, CPS

Albert Einstein said, "*The intuitive mind is a sacred gift, and the rational mind is a faithful servant. We have created a society that honors the servant and forgotten the gift.*" For much too long, the workforce has segregated the energies of their eternal spirit and that of their present human mind. The infinite wisdom of one's spirit continues to acquire knowledge eternally through life lessons from outer life experiences. It is an energy that lies within all and has a power beyond the mind's imagination. It is an energy just waiting to be recognized and utilized for success. By knowing and honoring our spirit, keeping our bodies healthy, maintaining a balance between heart and ego and opening our minds to infinite possibilities, we can tap into our intuition, a trustworthy GPS to life and success. The corporate transformation of minds and thinking patterns will change the desires of accomplishments. When the path to desired success is one that serves the highest good, the Universe shall conspire to manifest our desires producing prosperity, abundance and more successful careers and lives.

Outer life experiences whether positive or negative, have profound effects on the inner natural state of the spirit that can either elicit automatic reckless reactions OR well-thought-out responses. Those who allow outer life experiences to define their spirit and ultimately their ego get into the driver's seat and speed down the road of life close minded. What happens when we operate with a one-track mind? Success gets further and further down the road because the eyes of the soul can't read the signs of manifestation. One who has an acceptance of their outer life experiences and an understanding that they have no control over such can process their elicited emotions and have the humility to learn lessons from all.

Their outer life experiences then become an invitation to change. Their spirit is not only being accessed but also open to acquiring further wisdom. By becoming mindful of the ever evolving spiritual power within, they tap into their intuition which releases responses rather that quick, harsh reactions.

Becoming mindful of our spirit is to know who our spirit is. Our spirit is a sacred gift of energy. Everything is energy! When we need guidance, spirit is there whether it is ours or that of our loved ones who have passed to the spirit world. Spirit world energy is indestructible. Our energy, although limited by being encased human form is just as powerful. Spirit has an energetic intelligence that gently whispers. This cosmic intelligence is also known as intuition. Those living through ego never hear it. It is the one who begins to take on the practice of honoring their spirit, getting closer to it and knowing it that hears it. They hear it but don't always trust it. Trust comes from the consistent practice of getting closer to one's spirit and understanding who he/she is that enables intuition to speak louder and louder. Trust, confidence, and a relationship develops between us and our intuition. Mastering the volume is to become silent and sit in the power of your spirit. It is called meditation.

Those who maintain a meditation practice allowing their mind to open to their spirit hear answers to their life's questions. Meditation can be as intense or as light as one chooses. There are many forms of meditation that vary from a hardcore, one-hour silent meditation to moving meditation such as yoga or even 15-minutes walking barefoot in the grass. The answers aren't always blatantly definitive or written in stone. They don't always come easy. They may, but it is the open, tamed mind that catches the signs and symbols or hears it from the spirit world. In fact, the answers may come in many different forms. The answers may appear immediately, although not likely without a lifelong practice. The answers may come in the form of synchronistic moments validating that we are right where we are supposed to be, a song, an idea from inspiration or in an ah ha moment. A mantra from Jonathan Lockwood Huie demonstrates the philosophy and power behind mindful spirit. "I dream with powerful intention – opening my mind to spirit, I trust my intuition to deliver powerful visions of my inspired future, and empower my intent to transform those visions into reality."

The transformation that occurs from joining the mind with its spirit also depends upon the energetic balance of heart and ego. This is essential. There is no room for an abundance of ego when honoring the energy of spirit, here or hereafter. Ego causes problems while heart solves them. The mind should follow the heart, and the heart should follow the mind. It is a transcendence of consciousness. Human minds will always have symptoms of ego such as fear, anger, resentment, always wanting more, nasty, dominant, controlling, etc. Egos that run the show are of dominance. Lives being led by ego are such historical tyrants as Hitler, Saddam Hussein, and Mikhail Gorbachev. Most of all ego is made up of extreme selfishness. It displays thoughts and behavior of deceit. In the business world, trust and rapport crumble. The ego can also work against the spirit and become an energy vampire to others. To feel good, those who allow ego to govern their spirit need to feed themselves with the positive energy of others. Self-esteem can begin to dwindle. Working all the time sets in and begins to take over as the ego seeks and needs more and more approval and self-satisfaction. This domino effect brings the physical body to a place of tenseness, and a nervous state of mind. People who become stuck in the ego stage can find this a permanent state. The key to success is to keep ego in check and transition to heart-based consciousness. This balance is imperative not only to success but also physical well-being. Overworking and ego are too much negative energy for the human body, spirit, and mind to handle.

The entire shift of a corporate mind honoring its spirit, acknowledging eternal wisdom and infinite soul growth, developing and trusting its intuition, accepting life on life's terms and balancing ego with heart depends on and can only be done when maintaining a healthy physical body. Typically, the corporate mind that isn't in touch with all of these elements of their spirit isn't in touch with their health. It is a proven scientific fact that emotion, lack of movement and bad choices put into one's body causes physical pain and illness. Emotional thoughts are energy and have a major impact on the cells of the human body. Stresses of the workplace such as over thinking, anger, sadness, etc. squash the spirit, crush the heart and make the body ill. Plenty of rest, water, exercise, healthy food and time to play equals a healthy body. Health is an essential component to achieving optimum honor to the spirit. A healthy body, mind, and spirit enable a clear path with the clarity needed to harness success.

Finally, positive energy is successful energy. Our thoughts and intentions are energy. All this energy swirls around the Universe. As Madame Blavatsky once said, "Matter is spirit at its lowest level. Spirit is matter at its highest level." It is the spirit within that knows what earthly matter it wants to create and manifest. As it has been said, the skies the limit. If the energy of corporate world minds are willing to blend with the energy of their spirit, seek spiritual guidance from the spirit world, acknowledge their heart, tap into/listen/trust their intuition, accept outer life experiences as invitations for change, maintain a healthy physical body, and set intentions of positive thoughts, the Universe will conspire to make them successful beyond their imagination. "When I let go of what I am . . . I become what I might be," said Lao Tzu. The concepts of letting go of attachment, closed mindedness and expectations are outside of most people's comfort zone. It is a difficult task to undertake but having faith in one's spirit, the courage to seek inner truths, and the strength to let go of what was, makes room for what will be. When the energy has been put out into the Universe that one desires to experience ultimate success for the highest good for themselves and others, the law of attraction kicks in. What once may have seemed insurmountable begins to unfold with ease. Gratitude, contentment, and kindness radiate from within. Inspiration and new ideas open up where dead ends once laid. Success is on the horizon. The minds of corporate life shift anew and the workplace expands into infinity. By honoring their spirit, they harness their success and live their life purpose. They will achieve their highest potential of entrepreneurship or whatever their heart desires in this life. All they have to do is stand in the power of their spirit, live the truths of their heart and soul, and they attain new heights within their career, relationships and their resume of life and beyond, with love, light, and peace. Be guided by spirit not driven by ego.

About Deborah Livingston, SNUi, CPS

As seen on WBZ news and featured on the cover of OMTimes Magazine, Deborah Livingston is an award winning, International Psychic Medium, Animal Communicator, Author of Strand of Pearls, Mentor and a Shaman. Deborah has been attending the Arthur Findlay College in England annually where she takes mediumship course and is a member of the Spiritualist National Union. Deborah is a member of Shay Parker's Best American Psychics, listed on Bob Olson's best psychic medium directory and also chose as one of the Top Psychics in Boston by Jack Rourke, one of the most prominent professional psychics in North America. Deborah's service are private and small or large group readings, large venue galleries, workshops, fundraising and speaking.

Contact Deborah Today!

Website: http://www.deblivmedium.com

Phone: 617-817-0721

Email: Debliv11@gmail.com

Chapter 11

From Roadblocks to Discovering Results?

Authored by Cecelia "Fi" Mazanke

In January of 2000, the start of the new millennium was also when I embarked on an entirely new career path. After being in the corporate world for twelve years, I became a Leadership Coach, a venture that was a calling of my heart. My intentions were clear; I would help people create undeniably successful results. I committed to creating a company that would help clients achieve noticeable change.

My program was introduced to the leadership team at my former employer. I had complete belief and confidence people would volunteer to enroll in my coaching program. Through my own process of coaching, I learned to trust that the perfect people to get the results would enroll. I also believed beyond a shadow of a doubt, those people would be aligned to drive the program forward. Along with that trust and with a nervous excitement to start, I stepped into what would be my life's passion. With those clear intentions firmly established in my mind, I wasn't surprised as three people stepped forward to begin. The gratitude I feel for those three souls who trusted me in my new adventure is immeasurable. I have since learned when your destiny is calling, and you put forth an unwavering faith, outstanding results cannot help but follow.

In the corporate world, results are most often measured in numbers. I saw my coaching business in the same way, and the results I got from my first three clients were quantifiable. The bottom line sales and recruiting numbers improved. One leader, who carried a significant financial debt, cleared that debt and at the end of her coaching program, she had amassed $17,000 in savings. Even more amazing, though, were the peace of mind and a greater degree of happiness my clients expressed since they entered the program. To me as a coach, I felt tremendous satisfaction knowing my clients were getting measurable results, and they were feeling more empowered and more balanced as they continued to work with me.

To summarize the method to obtaining these results is a compilation of thousands of hours of working with clients, and observing myself, over the past twenty years. There are some consistent truths I want to share with you to empower you on your introspective journey through life. These truths apply in business, personal relationships, with young people and old, and no matter what the goal. I even worked with a young teen who was bullied in high school, and after two sessions, she manifested the results she desired. Anyone can benefit from this approach.

The main principle in my coaching technique to obtain consistent and lasting results is first to clear the road blocks that prevent one from achieving success. Those road blocks can be boiled down to one main topic, FEAR. Fear comes in many forms. It can appear as anxiety, depression, financial hardships, addiction, anger, grief, rage and the list goes on. You see, fear is not our natural state of existence; LOVE is our natural state. As you are traveling on the path of life, when you encounter an experience whereby you do not achieve your outcomes, you can look inward to find the block. The great news is that this process is not difficult, and you have the answer within yourself to release the block. The answer lies within your body.

Years ago, I was seeing a wise man named Dr. Martin Plotkin. He has since passed away, but we spent extra time in his office philosophizing and sharing deep discussions about life. Dr. Plotkin said one thing to me that will remain embedded in my mind. He said, "Fi, the body tells the truth always and forever." I thought to myself if the body tells the truth on a physical level, there is a possibility that it can work on an emotional level as well.

In my work with my clients, I found a consistent connection

112

between stuck emotions and lack of results. So, I began working with my clients to determine where inside their bodies they may be holding onto emotions. I used a technique designed by Brandon Bays called, "The Journey." The Journey helps clients uncover those hidden emotions that hold them back. I began to modify the process as I went along, based on my results and I found there was a connection between what clients experienced in the past and how the pattern is recreated for the purpose of healing in their current reality. I also noticed that by experiencing these road block emotions, giving them a voice and forgiving the people involved in the trauma, results magically happened. What I learned is positive affirmations and adjusting thoughts to align with the desired outcome were successful tools in coaching; however, more lasting results occurred once the emotion was identified, honored by giving it a voice and then forgiven. That is the process by which the client could actually see or feel a release within themselves.

There is a simple explanation for these profound results. As road blocks are released during the coaching process, we connect to what I call a "divine" source within us. You can think of it as our internal source of energy and flow. Neuropeptides within the body hold emotional experiences from the past and can block the divine source energy within the body. As clients explore and then release the road blocks within themselves, this life force energy flows more freely, and a greater level of connection to the divine source energy occurs.

I witnessed the most significant example of this with one of my clients years ago. He was an executive leader, and travel was required for his job. He suffered from anxiety and claustrophobia, particularly when he traveled. Planes and the backs of buses caused him such panic he wanted to jump right out of them. As we explored the road blocks in his body, we found he had a trip to the Emergency Room for a racing heart, due to a reaction to a supplement he was taking with cough medicine. In the ER, he was treated by a doctor and was in a semi-conscious twilight state. What we discovered was fascinating. While in the ER and when the doctor assumed he was not fully conscious, the doctor said some damaging words about my client. My client had no recollection of this experience until we explored the emotion held in his body. It was so devastating to my client that he stored that experience in his cellular memory and it became a roadblock to his success. When we allowed his voice to be expressed to that doctor, and then offered the doctor forgiveness, the road block was released. My client was then able to travel without the extreme panic he experienced prior to our session. He still felt anxiety while traveling, but it did not cause the debilitating outcome anymore.

I have found while some road blocks are directly connected to the lack of success, more often, there is an underlying less obvious connection that is revealed through work with the body. In the case of this client, he had unconsciously connected travel to the memory of his ER experience.

In another example, a client experienced a lack of success in her sales organization. Her father died when she was 15 years old. She was holding unexpressed grief in her left forearm. After her father had died, her family told her to be strong and keep busy. That advice was counterproductive to the flow of her life force energy connecting to her divine source. Once she had permission to empty out her grief, and offer forgiveness, she was able to feel relief, and we then introduced coaching tools for her to manifest success. Her sales skyrocketed, and she felt more joy and happiness in her life.

We often hear results come to those who work hardest. Through my coaching practice, I have found results come when people realize the answers are within them. Once clients eliminate roadblocks to success, they can open to the power of the gifts and talents they have to offer to the world. As people understand they are here to add value through their passions, they can fulfill their mission and serve others through their gifts. I use a resourceful tool called the Birkman® Method to clearly demonstrate a client's beautiful mosaic of interests, styles, and needs. In using the Birkman® Method, a client can see how their work or hobby can serve a higher purpose matching his special skill set. Their lives carry a much richer experience as they see how they can use their unique abilities for the benefit of humanity.

Outstanding results are easily attained as you experience each emotion rather than resisting it. Using the body as a means to realizing those roadblocks allows a discovery process that produces lasting results for success. All the best on your journey

to outstanding results!

About Cecelia "Fi" Mazanke

Cecelia "Fi" Mazanke has been empowering people through her Leadership Coaching program since the start of the millennium. Fi's unique method of discovering a person's road blocks to unveil their power of possibility supports sustainable success. The direct connection that occurs as a person remembers her greatness inspires success in all areas of life. The impact of Fi's coaching methods includes vastly improved business results, significantly enhanced personal relationships, and an overall feeling of fulfillment and life purpose. Through Fi's coaching practice, an increased level of client empowerment is the intention and the outcome achieved.

Fi began coaching in January of 2000. The program swept the nation with its outstanding results. Since then, Fi has supported tens of thousands of clients throughout North America to discover success and significantly change their lives for the better.

Contact Fi Today!

Email: fi@directconnectcoacing.com

Facebook: https://www.facebook.com/DirectConnectCoaching/

Chapter 12

Effective Communication through Exhibitions: Five Lessons and a Rule

Authored by Carol Bossert, Ph.D.

We usually associate exhibitions with museums or international expositions like the World's Fair. But many companies create exhibition experiences for their clients, whether it's a lobby display to commemorate achievements, a central location to introduce new products or a temporary presentation at a trade show. Exhibitions are a unique and powerful form of communication. They can generate a lasting impression and can even transform the way people think. But like any communication medium, there are rules of thumb and best practices that can enhance their effectiveness. Even a poorly executed exhibition can give a lasting impression...just not the one you want.

Why do an exhibition?

If you want to convey technical information, build a website. If you want to mount a detailed argument, write a book. But if you want to generate enthusiasm, empathy and even curiosity about your company, create an experience. Exhibitions are immediate, immersive and intimate, more akin to a live performance than a classroom.

An exhibition demands attention. It cannot be put aside to be read later. Audiences are surrounded by sights, sounds and even smells, and they are physically invested in their experience. They can build their understanding through touch and even taste. No two people experience an exhibition in exactly the same way. It is the ultimate personalized experience.

Lesson #1 – Understand Your Audience

One of the biggest mistakes that people make when planning an exhibition is believing—or wanting to believe—that their exhibition will hold universal appeal and should be designed for "everybody." In reality, an exhibition designed for everyone is good for no one. Why? Exhibitions are the result of a design process that generates solutions based on understanding the needs of an audience. The more information we have about the particular audience we are trying to reach, the better our decisions and the more effective the exhibition.

Understand your audience within the context of the exhibition experience. Will people encounter this exhibition in a lobby or waiting room? If so, what is their mindset? For instance, people in a hospital waiting room will have a very different set of concerns than customers visiting a corporate headquarters. Is your audience limited by time? Do they have only five minutes in a lobby before being whisked off to an interview? Are they in a convention hall with only a few minutes between sessions? What other activities are vying for their attention? Are they encountering the exhibit alone?

As a group? Does your audience want to be guided through the exhibitions or would they rather explore on their own?

Understanding your audience goes beyond understanding markets and demographics.

Know your audience well enough to give them a face and emotional attributes. An exhibition is a conversation. You don't have a conversation with a faceless entity. You have a conversation with a person who has interests, needs, experiences, fears and expectations. You need to understand your audience so that you know where and how to begin the conversation.

Beware of phrases like "Everybody will…" or "No one will…" Test these and all assumptions that you have made about your audience. Begin the conversation with your audience well before you start designing the exhibition.

Lesson # 2 – Define Your Objectives

National parks use visitor centers to equip their audiences with skills and knowledge to explore and appreciate the park's natural features. Similarly, an effective corporate visitor center can help potential clients understand the value of your products and services.

Exhibitions are not particularly effective at transmitting detailed information (aka facts), but in our networked world of smart devices, they don't need to. Exhibitions are best at creating moods, impressions, and ideas that can spark imagination and curiosity. Exhibitions can create lasting impressions that transform the ways in which people view themselves and the world they live in.

The key question in determining an overarching objective for your exhibition is, "What do you want your visitor to become?"

Visiting an exhibition will not result in an immediate action such as purchasing goods or services, but exhibition experiences can provide your audience with tools to help them appreciate the goods and services that affect their future decisions. A discount clothing retailer used the tagline, "Our best customer is an educated consumer." This organization knew that the more their customers knew about clothing, the more they could appreciate the value that this store provided. How do you define a good customer? What do they need to understand to appreciate your brand? How do your values connect with your audience's values?

Lesson # 3 – Have A Point of View

In other words, what does your exhibition taste like? Tastes are memorable. Clearly communicating your company's point of view is critical to creating a memorable exhibition. There is no such thing as a neutral experience. Don't be afraid of expressing yours. The most effective exhibitions have a point of view that is grounded in the organization's mission and is a reflection of their values. Using the conversation analogy again, visitors should know who they are talking to.

A company's point of view directly affects the narrative it tells. Everyone loves a good story, but stories alone are soon forgotten unless we can find meaning in them. A narrative is a thread that holds individual stories together and gives them meaning. The narrative connects someone else's stories to our own and, by extension to the broader human experience. The story of the company founder is just a jumble of facts until it is grounded in a larger human narrative.

Lesson #4 – Be Interactive

Conversations are interactive; one person reacts to another person. An effective exhibition is an interaction between the organization and its audience. Make sure that your exhibition is not one sided. Ask your audience for their opinions. Get them involved. Listen.

Interactivity is not about the use of specific technologies. It is about giving the audience choice and letting them chart their own path and make the experience their own. A major misunderstanding is that something like looking at a painting is a non-interactive experience. This could not be further from the truth. Looking at something may not seem like much on the outside, but on the inside, it is mental gymnastics. The art of really looking builds curiosity. An effective exhibition helps people learn how to look.

Effective exhibits leave room for the visitor to participate.

Lesson # 5 - Beware Unintended Messages

Even well-designed and polished exhibitions can communicate unintended messages to audiences. Here are a few of the most common.

Location, Location, Location

Is your exhibition featured prominently and proudly in a central location or is it in an ill-lit and obscure location, perhaps a hallway that few people use? If the latter, the exhibition says, "We don't really care about this and neither should you."

Words Matter

Much has been written about labels in exhibitions. Research has shown that even people with a very high level of interest in a topic, will only read 50 words before stopping. So knowing that, why would an exhibition contain large panels or screens filled with words? Aside from telegraphing that the organization did not spend enough time thinking clearly about what it wanted to say, text-heavy exhibitions tell the audience, "We really don't care whether you read any of this or not."

Don't Weigh It Down

Sometimes an exhibition is sunk by the sheer weight of the objects and images it includes. Organizations with rich archives are lucky, but if they decide to display .everything without clear organization or focus, the audience is left wondering what is important. In effect the organization is saying, "We don't know either, can you figure it out?"

Think Hospitality

You treat your potential clients as guests. You offer them refreshments and make sure they know where the restrooms are. Don't abandon this hospitality in the exhibition hall. Provide adequate seating—and when your architect says there is adequate seating, add some more. Make sure restrooms are readily available and clearly marked. Assure that light levels are adequate. If not, the exhibition says, "We don't care enough about you to make you comfortable."

Remove Obstacles

A barrier can be as obvious as a table that blocks access to a space, or as subtle as the use of industry jargon. Look at the exhibition through a guest's eyes. If obstacles are left unnoticed, you may be saying, "Get out. This is not for you."

The Rule

All these lessons boil down to one rule: Practice empathy. There may be many reasons why your company wants to create an exhibition, but unless you clearly understand the needs, expectations, and experiences of your target audience your exhibition will not communicate effectively and could even backfire. Respect your audience and begin a conversation that can last a lifetime.

About Carol Bossert, Ph.D.

Carol has loved museums since she was 6 years old when her mother took her to the Field Museum of Natural History to see the dinosaurs and dioramas. There she experienced a sense of awe and curiosity about nature that led to an advanced degree in biology and eventually a job in a museum where she created magical moments for others to enjoy.

In 1998, Carol started her own business to apply her skills and knowledge in exhibition development to the needs of an ever-growing set of clients interested in connecting with audiences in new and memorable ways. Carol helps her clients present their own stories through corporate visitor centers and temporary displays.

Contact Carol today!

Website: http://carolbossertservices.com/

Email: carol.bossert@verizon.net

LinkedIn: https://www.linkedin.com/in/carolbossert

Twitter: https://twitter.com/musewrite

Chapter 13

The Path to Sustainable Results

Authored by Cibele Salviatto, PCC

The day I left my fancy office, and resigned from my six-figure job was a typical grayish and cloudy day in the city of Sao Paulo. I was a director in a prominent Venture Capital company during the start-up boom in Brazil, and my job seemed to be just perfect. My boss was as astonished and surprised as I was with my resignation. And yet, a feeling of relief engulfed me. It was 2001, and I was free to follow my real path.

Eleven years earlier, I had graduated as a business administrator and started working in the financial industry as an investment analyst. Although that was not a passion, it worked well for me; in ten years, I climbed the ladder from an investment analyst to a leadership position. Those years provided a solid professional foundation, sharpened my analytical skills, and gave me the luxury of knowing, in relative depth, a handful of different industries.

In spite of my successful career, I was not happy. I sensed that life should be more than making money and being perceived as successful. I needed to give back the gifts I've received from life, to contribute to something larger. That was when I found Pathwork.

Pathwork is a path of self-development strongly based on self-acceptance and self-responsibility. It is an invitation to question our thoughts, observe our emotions and to go deeper into the conscious and unconscious beliefs that rule our lives. And, as a spiritual path, it guides us to a broader reality of who we are, one that encompasses the possibility of transcendence of our egos and integration of the dualities that split us apart on a daily basis.

Guided by Pathwork, I journeyed to the innermost part of my being; I became more grounded and secure, being able to make moves outwardly that were more aligned with the calls of my heart and soul. Nearly two years after I started Pathwork, I was able to have that conversation with my boss and begin a new journey as a sustainability consultant. In 2001, "Atitude" (as it is written in Portuguese) a consulting company in Corporate Sustainability, was born.

As defined by a report released in 1987 by the World Commission on Environment called our Common Future, sustainability is a development that "seeks to meet the needs and aspirations of the present without compromising the ability to meet those of the future." Specifically in the business context, sustainability is the ability to manage a corporation by finding a proper balance between its various stakeholders' needs and desires. It implies putting together opposite interests, accommodating different perspectives and finding ways to creatively deal with divergences and conflicts among employees, community, society, environment, clients, suppliers, and shareholders. It is challenging and complex.

Along the way, I had an experience that changed the course of my life once again. I was attending a sustainability retreat, talking to my dear friend and physician Dr. Fernando Bignardi, about plans and ideas of how to "save the planet" and to "help the nature." Dr. Fernando was listening to me with that peaceful countenance, typical of wise people when he softly said, "Yes, but WE ARE NATURE." In a matter of seconds, those words transformed my work. At that moment I realized in deeper levels of my consciousness, there is no "saving the planet, or helping nature" as if planet or nature were something else apart from myself. I comprehended that the notion of a subject separated from an object is a big illusion. I learned that to be more effective in my professional objectives, I would need to integrate the same principles I was living in my personal development journey.

Working with sustainability was a way of following the deepest calling of my heart. Pathwork, or, in other words, the deep understanding of my own emotional, mental and spiritual being has made it possible. Both together are helping me realize the fragmented mechanistic Newtonian-Cartesian-Darwinian patriarchy society within which we all live has not only been ruling and shaping our individual and group lives for ages, but it is also the real cause of our unsustainable world. It is the cause of our frustration, loneliness, and lack of sustainable results in our life. Why? Because it maintains us in the illusion that things are not interconnected. It misinforms our mindset and leads us to perform actions disconnected from the whole. And because the reality is systemic, integrated, interconnected and interweaved, when we act in the world with a fragmented mindset, the results we achieve do not last or fulfill us. Sooner or later we experience an undesired unseen consequence that is caused by this disconnection.

In 2009, I left Brazil and moved to the US. I intuitively knew it would be very difficult to maintain my activities as a sustainability consultant here, but it was the perfect situation for me to develop a path that would drive us to more sustainable results, a path of challenging mindsets. I still needed a structure and a language that better suited the corporate world and also those who do not identify themselves with a spiritual path. I found that in Integral Coaching Canada (ICC). As a coaching method inspired by and focused on Ken Wilber's Integral Vision, ICC brought me the framework I needed to create Sustainability from Within.

Sustainability from Within is an approach that integrates the various learning and experiences I've had so far and helps those looking for lasting results. It provides a path to open up the mind for transcendence of the obstacles and hindrances that keep us stagnated or unfulfilled.

Sustainability from Within is based on two great pillars:

1. From duality to unity

If the linear and fragmented mindset is the cause of unsustainable results, we need a path that provides the tools for us to move from a dualistic perspective of the word to a more unitive model. Duality is the inherent home of our egos. It is how we see the world from the illusion of separateness. In duality we can't help experimenting everything as a matter of either/or. There is no good without bad, no pretty without ugly, no right without wrong.

Unity is the desired stage in which we perceive we not only have more in common with each other but that in fact, we are one. We are one with nature! A unitive state of consciousness is the inclusion of possibilities, the integration of apparent opposites. It calls for a change in the lens through which we see ourselves and the world.

The path from duality to unity includes an evolutionary process in which we are asked to develop a perspective that grows out of an egocentric perspective towards a globocentric perspective, as figure 1 suggests.

2. Self-responsibility

One of the immediate results of the duality/unity questioning is the awareness of self-responsibility. In the illusion of separateness, we end up in an endless blaming game that undermines our power. We look for and eventually find perpetrators everywhere in our daily life: in the traffic, in the economy, in the government, in our work

The evolution path

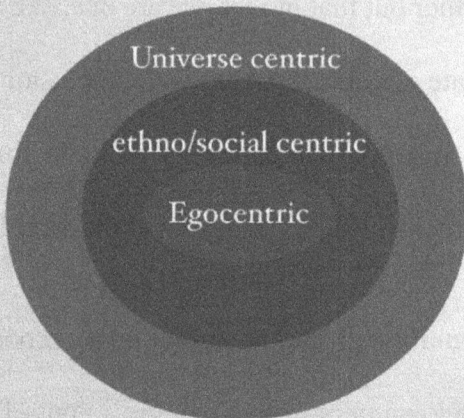

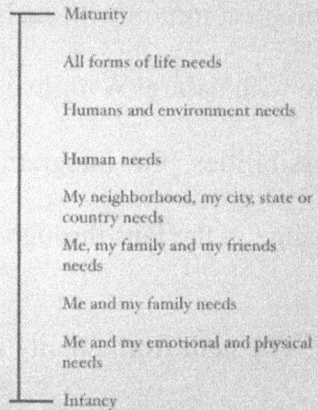

Universe centric

ethno/social centric

Egocentric

Maturity

All forms of life needs

Humans and environment needs

Human needs

My neighborhood, my city, state or country needs

Me, my family and my friends needs

Me and my family needs

Me and my emotional and physical needs

Infancy

Based on Ken Wilber's integral Vision and Pathwork

environment, in our house. We may not like to assume that, but deep down, we believe we are powerless victims. By moving out of duality towards a more integrative approach, we gain power and may envision new unseen possibilities.

Thus, in pursuing a more sustainable result, from our Sustainability from Within approach, one must:

1. Identify the either/or in the situation you are dealing with. Recognize the dual nature of goals, objective, intentions and conflicts and question yourself: is there a possibility of a both/and approach? What would be a more "evolved" solution or approach given the maturity path scale that we proposed in figure 1?

2. Stop the blaming game. Whenever you find yourself in a victim position, challenge yourself: what in this situation can be positive? What did I contribute for that to happen? What can I do to envision a more integrated reality?

3. Develop a self-observer. Learn to observe yourself, your thoughts and emotions. Self-observation is of paramount importance to catch the subtleties of our fragmented minds. Our emotional reactions, the words we use, the thoughts our minds think are all indications of our real beliefs and intentions, even if they are not flattering to us or point to something we'd rather not see about ourselves.

4. Accept that as humans, we are imperfect. Paradoxically, only by acknowledging and accepting our imperfections will we be able to transform them. Judging and hiding are only

other facets for blaming and victimization which keeps us in the duality sphere and thus, in illusion.

5. Question your thoughts, your beliefs, your usual way of doing things. Question your motives, your intentions. Give the other side of duality a chance, and by that, you increase your chances of overcoming it.

Only by questioning and facing our darkness will we be able to fully express our light. Only by acknowledging we live in a world of duality and understanding how this is the root of our unsustainable results, will we be able to be more efficient. Choosing integration and inclusion will provide you with the tools you need to follow a path towards more sustainable results. Let's try it?

About Cibele Salviatto, PCC

Cibele has been contributing with large corporations' sustainability strategy and implementation for 15 years while offering her sensibility, intuition and knowledge to boost her individual coach client's self-development and spiritual path. Her passion is to promote "Sustainability from Within" which is a comprehensive body or work that includes self-discovery and self-development as a way to improve the effectiveness of her clients' actions. She assists them in refining their vision, deepening their intentions and becoming more aware of the causes and effects that are ruling their present lives, opening for sustainable transformation to take place. If you want to enhance the effectiveness of your impact in the world, contact Cibele Salviatto

Contact Cibele Today!

Websites: http://www.cibelesalviatto.com

Email: cibelesalviatto@me.com

Phone: 305-505-4743

Twitter: http://twitter.com/cibelesalviatto

Facebook: https://www.facebook.com/cibelesal/ and

https://www.facebook.com/pathworkinflorida/

LinkedIn: https://www.linkedin.com/in/cibelesalviatto

Chapter 14

Outstanding Doctor–Patient Relationships: How to Connect with your Physician and Receive Optimal Care

Authored by Debra Wickman, MD, MS, FACOG

I came of age in the 1970's and following high school, chose from the three basic career paths deemed acceptable for a girl – teacher, secretary or nurse. With an affinity for science and a nurturing personality, I chose nursing without hesitation. The most important gift nursing gave me was comfort and ease in communicating with patients one on one. It was as a nurse I learned how to explain medical situations to patients and saw the frustration when they didn't have enough information or lacked clarity in goals and expectations of treatment. I experienced death and dying up close learning to lean into the experience and truly provide support, rather than avoiding or preempting any display of emotion.

I was single and had an insatiable thirst for learning and new experiences. It was on a family skiing vacation in Telluride, Colorado, the trajectory of my life took a major turn. I was riding the chairlift with my uncle, the father figure in my life. I had been the flower girl at his wedding to my aunt, and have always felt a special bond with him. It was not unusual to receive life lessons and advice from him, so I was not surprised when he began sharing observations about my life. He asked me: "If money was no concern, and you could do anything you want with your life what would you choose?" I reflect on that moment now as nothing short of miraculous, and a giant boost toward connecting me with my life path. What a precious opportunity, at the age of twenty-five, to be offered that query, backed by the love and sincerity to follow it up. I answered, "I would go to medical school." My aunt and uncle gave me an interest-free loan to pursue my dream of becoming a physician, and after taking two years of necessary pre-requisite courses, the MCAT exam and jumping through the hoops of the medical school admissions process, I found myself enrolled in the University of Washington, School of Medicine.

Delayed Gratification and the Feminine Psyche

Medical school was a blissful experience, providing state of the art learning opportunities, in an atmosphere set up for success. Post-graduate residency training in obstetrics and gynecology built on that foundation, with a demanding schedule, and amazing academic and clinical learning experiences. It was an all-encompassing, 24/7 whirlwind, and I loved it. The reality of that span, however, is I don't remember doing anything else! I missed many family events and was too busy or distracted to pay attention to many details in the lives of those I cared about. I would like to have had romance, or even dates! But began my mantra of "later," and "after I'm done with Ob-Gyn training," to assuage any pangs of loneliness or missing out.

I find this to be a common theme among women – one doesn't have to enroll in medical school to experience this. It shows up in the subtle voice that tells us we can wait until later to enjoy life; wait until the kids are in college to deal with our stale relationship; wait until I lose 20 pounds to feel happy. This mantra can easily become a pattern that defeats our ability to be happy in the "now." It's a pattern I recognize in my patients and find great benefit in helping women find ways to enjoy life's current condition.

A Career Caring for Women

After residency, I started a career in private practice obstetrics and gynecology. I thrived on the connection in the continuity of caring for women through all stages of life. It did not take long for patients to feel enough trust to start asking me questions about intimate issues, concerns about sexual function and desire. I realized my training, like that in most Centers, prepared me well for dealing with medical crises, and offering evidence-based medical care, but I had little training in female sexuality, so needed to explore this mysterious but ubiquitous topic.

I enrolled in a unique post-graduate fellowship program at University of California, Los Angeles, in Female Sexual Medicine. It was a fascinating year, devoted to learning techniques in diagnostic testing, and hormonal therapy, research, and vaginal surgery. Female sexual medicine is a new field in terms of medical specialty, with few FDA-approved therapies, and rare evidence-based techniques and procedures. The body of work is growing, with more research-based findings relevant to women each year. And this became my specialty, the complete care for women which involves more than the physical body, but the psychosexual being consisting of body/mind/heart and spirit. In the close relationship I establish with my patients, I have come to understand how important honesty and trust is to any patient/physician relationship.

How to Develop an Optimal Relationship with your Physician

All relationships are founded on trust, and the one with your doctor is no exception. I find the most rewarding interactions are with patients who I have known over time, through many experiences. Patients are often unaware of the steps they can take to foster their relationship with their doctor. I have been an obstetrician/gynecologist for more than twenty years, and have observed some consistent trends that positively influence this rapport.

1. Be organized for your appointment.

Make it easy and efficient for your physician to help you. Arrange prior records, lab results and radiology reports in a folder you bring to the appointment. Ideally, make a copy for the doctor to keep. A great deal of time is spent requesting prior records and chasing down laboratory reports when that time could be used to efficiently discuss the paperwork you have in-hand.

2. Be prepared to participate in your care.

Optimal wellness takes place when a patient integrates guidance from the doctor into daily life practice. It is never so simple as to take a pill or undergo a procedure. Ask what else can be done, or what other options are possible to improve outcome. I encourage patients to keep a list of questions to bring to the appointment. For follow-up appointments, it helps to keep a log of events/responses either on a paper calendar or in a smartphone, for easy correlation.

3. Optimal wellness may involve some out-of-pocket expenses.

I frequently encounter the mindset that all health-related expenses should be covered by insurance. Increasingly, treatments or therapies may not be covered, or practitioners who provide specialized expertise may not be contracted with insurance. The point is that priorities and options need to be discussed with your doctor. Embrace the underlying philosophy that you are worth the cost of paying for treatment that will assist with getting your optimal results.

4. Set realistic expectations.

Get clarity about what to expect from prescriptions or treatment recommendations. Realize few results are achieved instantly and with no effort. Ask what time frame is typical to experience the desired effect, and what else you can do to enhance the outcome.

5. Be proactive.

Be assertive and timely about following up. If something is not progressing as was described, don't hesitate to return for updated advice. Momentum is lost when too much time passes between appointments, especially if a prescription expires, or a regimen lapses. Consistency is key for optimal health. I encourage my patients to be honest with me about all they are doing including the supplements, herbs, and treatments they are taking. I want to know all the practitioners they are consulting, books they are reading, and workshops they are attending − what works and what doesn't. Health care is optimal when the community is connected, and it helps me to learn about new ideas and possibilities as well.

6. Don't take my word for it – check your facts.

I think it is dangerous for a patient to give unquestioning power away to an authority figure. While you need to trust your physician, it is also reasonable to ask her to explain recommendations and show research evidence to back it up. Exploring material from other sources and sharing those concepts is a great way to spark dialogue and encourage new treatment ideas.

Optimal health care involves choosing your physician to be an ally in navigating the individualized path to your wellness. The better your doctor knows you, the easier it will be. The doctor's role is more than a technician and includes joining the wellness community needed to accomplish your goals. Look for a doctor who is linked with other resources, and happy to talk about them. I am a doctor because I have a passion for connecting with women to achieve optimal health, and empowering them toward more joyful, fulfilled lives.

About Debra Wickman, MD, FACOG

Debra Wickman, MD, MS, FACOG, is a gynecologist certified by the American Board of Obstetrics and Gynecology. She heads Female Sexual Medicine, Vulvar Medicine and Menopause Services in the Department of Obstetrics and Gynecology at Banner University Medical Center – Phoenix, and is a clinical faculty member of University of Arizona College of Medicine – Phoenix. She completed a fellowship in Female Sexual Medicine at UCLA, and is also a sexuality counselor, AASECT certification pending.

Her model of diagnosis and treatment incorporates programs that uniquely educate, empower, and encourage personal growth, sexual discovery and healing for women. The programs look beyond a singular medical, pharmaceutical, or behavioral therapy, and instead integrate all approaches from a mind-body perspective. Central to her model is a holistic sexuality approach, using her training as a gynecologist to link the physical aspect of healing with the mental, emotional and spiritual facets to treat the whole sexual being.

Contact Debra Today!

Website: drdebrawickman.com

Email: info@drdebrawickman.com

Facebook: Debra Wickman, MD, FACOG

Twitter: @DrDebraWickman

Linked In: Debra Wickman

Office Address:

Banner University Medical Center – Phoenix
Women's Institute
1441 North 12th Street
3rd Floor
Phoenix, AZ 85006

Office Phone: 602-521-5700

Chapter 15

CHANGE: The Beauty or the Beast?
How to Leverage Change to Rise to the Top

Authored by Carol Kelly, MS, CPC

"It is not the strongest of the species that survive, nor the

most intelligent, but the one most responsive to change."

-Charles Darwin

Let's reflect.

Thomas Paine once said, **"These are the times that try men's souls."** So I want to begin with a few questions…

- Are you a leader of an organization, department, or team, where people look to you for direction, guidance, and support?

- In the face of this, have you experienced some rapid, unexpected, disruptive, continuous changes?

- Did you choose these changes or did they just happen to you?

- Do you feel "stuck," frustrated, and stressed because you don't know what to do or you have tried some things and keep getting the same results?

With accelerated change, overwhelming complexities, and tremendous competition, both domestically and globally, the odds are that you could answer "yes" to at least one of these questions.

Now, let's project.

- If you could wave a magic wand and get the results you're looking for, what would they be?

- What impact would this have on your life and the lives of those who look to you for your leadership?

> ***Many are called, but few are chosen.***

-Ancient Proverb

If you are in a position of leadership or aspire to be, if you are the person people look to, it is more than likely that you did not choose leadership, leadership chose you. Now more than ever, these are the times that are calling for transformative, epic leadership. Now is the time for "chosen" leaders to rise to the top and be the catalysts for producing outstanding results in themselves and others.

Could it be that you are one of them? What does it take to be chosen?

Let's explore this. It does not require you to have an impressive title or be at the highest ranks in a company or organization. All that it requires is for you to accept the "call" and adhere to its conditions. Will you?

As a consultant, coach, and inspirational speaker for thousands of leaders over the past three decades, I have empowered them to be skillful in many core competencies that have, over the years, fulfilled the requirements to be an effective leader. However, in these times of massive, unprecedented change, I have found that is not enough. For those leaders who want to be set apart and rise to the top, there is one fundamental principle they must follow and two major characteristics they must also possess.

THE PRINCIPLE: You must change the way you (and others) think about change.

Change is paradoxical.

A paradox is something with contradictory qualities or phases. In nature, paradox doesn't exist because everything moves naturally from stage to stage. The paradox is created by the way human beings conceptualize, analyze and perceive change. We often see change as a "double bind" in which we are caught in an illusion of alternatives. We will instinctively try to make meaning of the change or to create some sense of understanding or familiarity, i.e.

it's either good or bad, positive or negative, to be embraced or resisted. Such "double-binds" result in friction, frustration, and conflict because neither view of change is a viable solution and actually perpetuates a problem because one or the other viewpoint will dominate depending on the environment or context.

One common example: Organizations have a tendency to develop and institutionalize their own pattern of thinking regarding ways to approach problems. This is often called "group think." When this pattern of thinking no longer serves the organization, by becoming repetitive and unproductive, it becomes necessary to think "outside" the established patterns.

Another example: When we, as individuals, cannot make meaning of the change, we become reactive and create our own "story" – "first this happened, now this will happen," or "that means (or leads to) this…" And the result looks like this:

RESULTS = No Results + A Good Story

Change is what you make it – the beauty or the beast.

Rewrite your story. Instead of locking into one viewpoint, shift to a higher logical level of thinking which lifts the situation out of the double bind placing it in a different frame that expands the range of possibilities. Reflect on the ways change has made you stronger, better, wiser, more focused. What opportunities did it present? What lessons did you learn? Change your thinking, and you change your world.

"When you rule out the impossible, everything can be believed, thereby making available a limitless and infinite array of new possibilities."

-Albert Einstein

Once when conducting a workshop with a group of newly promoted senior leaders, I asked the usual question of "what do you expect to get from this program?" One woman raised her hand and gave the most poignant answer to that question I had ever encountered. Through her answer, I knew she was well on her way to becoming a transformative leader. She answered, "I want to know why anyone would willingly follow me."

This leads me to share with you the two characteristics of an epic, transformative leader.

EMOTIONAL INTELLIGENCE

This term, popularized by Daniel Goleman, is defined as the ability to:

- Recognize, understand and manage our own emotions

- Recognize, understand and influence the emotions and well-being of others

In practical terms, this means being self-aware. As a leader, it means being aware that emotions can drive your behavior and impact people (positively and negatively). It means learning how to manage these emotions—both your own and others—especially when you are under pressure.

Examples of high-pressure situations that must be effectively dealt with—now more than ever—to be a transformative leader include:

- Making tough decisions

- Dealing with change and life transitions

- Dealing with setbacks, failure, and burnout

- Dealing with challenging relationships

- Dealing with conflict and highly charged, difficult conversations

For example, it is not the same to resolve a conflict based on mere facts vs. solving a conflict based on facts that have been influenced by an unawareness of one's and others' emotions and misunderstandings. I have found the former approach to be futile and the latter approach transformative. The emotional balance of a person in a position of power is critical to the well-being of the organization, department, or team.

INSPIRED GREATNESS

Practice what you preach. It's not what you say; it's what you do that's important. People are inspired by what they see, not just what they hear about. It's your practice of your policies (what people see and experience), not just your discussion of them that inspires people. Additionally, transformational leadership requires changing not only the way you think and act, but also the way you show your authenticity – the innermost core of who you are. This is a game-changer.

Inspire greatness, one team at a time. Build strong, resilient teams and incite them to do something great in the direction the organization wants to go. Find and speak to their strengths, not their weaknesses. Engage rather than criticize. Instill hope where there is fear, and power where there is pain. Encourage and facilitate constructive conflict and disagreements rather than avoid it.

I have had the pleasure of empowering many leaders to do this and witnessing their transformation.

FINAL THOUGHTS

The last word on this important subject takes us back to our initial thought by Charles Darwin (some research suggests it was Leon C. Megginson). *"It is not the strongest of the species that survive, nor the most intelligent, but the one most responsive (or adaptable) to change."*

What is meant by this? People can be unstoppable when they're in their comfort zone, dealing with the familiar, but when something significant changes and the leader or organization can't adapt fast enough, they will fail no matter how strong or intelligent they are. When something big happens, everyone has to adapt to survive.

This is an illustration of what the real imperative is for a leader today. But like most things in business and life, rapid change is a two-edged sword—a threat but also an opportunity, the beast but also the beauty.

Adapt. **Turn change into an opportunity**. When you look in the mirror, what do you see? Can you see only what you've done so far, or the issues and challenges you face, or your failures? Or do you see all the endless possibilities before you? Do you see hope and a brighter future for you and the ones you lead? When you think this way, it sets the tone for the rest of the organization, the department, or the team. When you are committed to your own growth, you'll get followers that are committed to their growth.

So embrace change! Be the leader people look to! Rise to the top! And may the Force be with you.

About Carol Kelly, MS, CPC

CAROL KELLY is a Change and Leadership expert known for providing innovative, transformative solutions that have empowered her clients to achieve results they never thought were possible. Her clients include Senior Leaders in proactive, progressive companies and professional organizations across diverse industries. Many of them describe her as "The Miracle Worker."

This is what one senior leader said about her: *"Carol is one of the most skilled, inspirational speakers that I have experienced. She's not only talented, she's gifted."*

Carol has three decades of experience as a passionate OD Consultant, Certified Professional Coach, and Keynote Speaker. Her background includes two key areas: first, two decades inside a Fortune 500 company and then as the founder of her own consulting firm. She has lived in both worlds.

She is an alumnae of the Indiana University Graduate School of Business and has been certified by, and partnered with, several internationally acclaimed consulting firms.

Contact Carol Today!

Website: http://www.distinctsolutionsctc.com

Email: carol@distinctsolutionsctc.com

LinkedIn: https://www.linkedin.com/in/carolkelly7

Twitter: https://www.twitter.com/carolctc7

Facebook: https://www.facebook.com/distinctsolutionsllc

Instagram: https://www.instagram.com/carolkellyspeaks

Chapter 16

Growing Your Contacts to Grow Your Business

Authored by Brenda Stanton

There are many proven ways to grow a business, but one of the most sustainable ways is by growing your contacts. Random dialing has created a very ugly stigma in society and has given rise to the dreaded telemarketer. Most people fail to realize there are dread and fear on both ends of the line; the telemarketer hates to make the call, and the customer hates receiving it.

I worked in the insurance industry, and our industry most certainly contributed to the reason telemarketing eventually became a four letter word. In insurance, you were literally, "dialing for dollars." The proof was in the numbers. Daily, we were told to schedule enough appointments for each week, you had to put in enough "dials" the previous week. For many years, even today, it's the industry standard for success. You were trained by the best sales gurus of the time on various sales methods. We attended sales seminars for three days every quarter for years and were dazzled by wildly successful top agents that were trotted across the stage touting that their success was a result of the "numbers."

The top sales manager at the time, who actually ended up being my sales manager, talked about how he locked himself in a hotel room over a weekend with nothing but a phone book until he booked enough appointments for the next two weeks. He did this mainly because everything outside of that room created too much of a distraction, and he included his own family in that group of distractors. He said it worked so great the first time he did it, it became his go-to method to book his appointments. Subsequently, he became the number one branch manager in the company.

But that was then, and this is now. Things have changed. And to be truthful, things actually changed because the feds stepped in and passed the "Do not call" laws which made it illegal to call a consumer if their name was on the national and state "do not call" registry. This law was a game changer; it's pretty sad we had to go there, but now that we have, I think most people will agree it is for the best. Consumers are happier, and it does not affect business-to-business calling or relationships with established clients.

Over time, the internet has also become a game changer. Initially, not many companies used the internet to make sales because few customers trusted it for business transactions. Internet security helped to build trust, so eventually, more and more businesses began investing in websites where they could direct their old and new customers to find information and shop. As a result, people began to shop the internet more consistently for at first minor, then later, major purchases. The internet in general and social media, in particular, has become a smorgasbord for anyone in sales because of the unprecedented access it gives to potential clients − often without even a phone call made.

But, this begs the question: "Similar to other sales mediums out there, where business transactions take place, how long will it remain unregulated?" Most of us can answer that question pretty accurately − It will remain that way until it becomes abused by unscrupulous and unethical salespeople. Public outcry demands regulatory laws that protect their privacy. What will that look like? A national "Do not click" list you opt into perhaps?

To avoid (or at the very least, slow down) such an idea, which would adversely affect all of us that make a living primarily on the internet, it's incumbent on every individual and business that share cyberspace to improve on the methods they use to approach clients continually. One way of doing this is using call lists. These lists are fine, especially when they are compiled by a trustworthy company that does their research, and can provide you with a targeted list. How you handle that client after the initial contact is critical because nobody wants to feel they are just a number or they were robo-dialed. If they perceive that thought, the conversation will be very short.

In my many years of marketing and sales, it has been my experience that people decide within the first 60 seconds (or less) whether or not they want to talk to you, so how they are approached is everything. When people are approached on a human level without all the salesy stuff, they will respond to you on that same level and will usually even hear you out! It's amazingly accurate how that works. Even people you may have nothing in common with, will respect the idea that you approach them as an individual, and not as a residual income prospect. As society changes and the internet evolves, the etiquette of approaching prospects is also evolving and morphing.

Our society has become so self-absorbed, many people have lost sight of basic interpersonal skills. Somewhere along the way, we have seriously gotten off track. But regardless of whether we are off or on, one old sales adage has and never will change, "the customer is always right." When the basic tenets of respect and good manners are observed, the payoff is clear in the form of closing more deals and getting great referrals as "gravy." When clients are happy, and they like you and what you have done for them, they will refer other's to you, making your job a lot easier.

Social Media is also a game changer. Have you noticed how so many people practically live their entire lives on social media?

Personally, I've noticed how some people spend all day long posting on Facebook (especially). What began with Facebook has evolved into too many social media apps to count, people literally cannot get away from it, especially with more and more mobile apps. There is a mobile app for anything you need to do or say in life. Unless you are considering a Facebook business page strictly confined to commerce, the public has to wade through so much social, personal "fluff," it's hard to see how Facebook could be very useful in business. This is true for Twitter as well and indicates attention spans are way too short. By far, the best social media business app for me is Linkedin.

Thankfully, Linkedin has a much higher standard for members, and it is a serious business platform. It's the best way to approach prospects for business. Obviously, Linkedin has put some serious effort into creating its great reputation. It's basically a cyberspace "water cooler." People are relaxed, more open to talking to you and hearing whatever it is you have to say or offer.

As a marketer and publicist, I often reflect on how things once were compared to how sales happen today with the new normal created by the internet. Most of our lives are spent offline so to speak, but our online lives are beginning to compete for a larger portion of that real estate. Even with, or maybe because of, the semi-obscurity and masking of people on the internet, people are − and rightfully so − more suspicious as to why you are contacting them. With Linkedin, you can build business relationships and contacts in a great way, either through introductions by others or invitation. Either way, it breaks the ice. Facebook is somewhat similar so far as inviting contacts, but there are far more random people on Facebook whereas Linkedin is a far more targeted business platform.

General observation shows many small businesses aren't as active on LinkedIn because of time and resources. But, to grow your business, you need an online presence to build a reputation and to earn new business. The old days of the hard sell are over. When you talk to people today, you need to be honest and upfront because your contact can google you while they are on the phone and find out anything they need to know about you. They can make a decision before the conversation is ever over as to whether or not they want to do business with you; it's that fast and effective. It's also the main reason you want to keep your information up-to-date. Information moves quickly, and if you have inaccurate information posted about either yourself or your business, it can kill your chances of success.

Today, job one is to make your prospects feel comfortable talking to you and for you to impress upon them that without a doubt, you are who they should be talking to because your competition is literally just a 'click' away. One bi-product of total access is short attention spans. Everyone is busy; time is at a premium for us all. We have so many great forms of communication in this century and should respect them.

About Brenda Stanton

Brenda Stanton is someone with a real knack for getting things done from a marketing perspective. Brenda has had a long and illustrious career in marketing, and sales management. Her clients have included Fortune 500 companies and many C-suite executives across many industries along with a top-level marketing guru in Silicon Valley, CA. Brenda has trained multitudes of sales managers and agents in the US and abroad in her techniques and skill set.

She believes her success lies in her genuine personality and attitude but says her greatest attribute has been her ability to open doors as a facilitator. Since she is so friendly and approachable, people enjoy talking to her, plus her Southern charm doesn't hurt! "One of the most important reasons for my success," Brenda explains, "is the confidence I display to others. It's a real confidence I feel, not out of arrogance, but out of the pride, I feel representing a product or brand I truly believe in. I continually pray to God for wisdom."

Currently, Brenda is Publicist for Jean Oursler and Alden Consulting in New Jersey, and she is International Publicist for WBTVN Women's Broadcast Television Network in Los Angeles, CA.

Contact Brenda Today!

Email: sparkleforaliving@gmail.com

Chapter 17

Beneficent Life Recipe

Authored by Wanda Harris

One might think of cake, a type of food or beverage when they hear the word "Recipe." But I have a new word alert: A Life Recipe. You may be saying to yourself who, why, how and what for? We can't possibly need a recipe for life when we are already living it. Newsflash: we do! In fact, when we mix up all of life's ingredients that becomes our recipe. We already know what the ingredients are and what brings the recipe into existence. For a cake, you have the batter, butter, icing, etc. and that is the recipe. When your taste buds require something else, or you want to excite your guests for dinner you scroll through recipes until you feel satisfied, and underneath that satisfaction is inspiration, creativity, and pleasure.

How many times do we have memory lapses about ingredients of our life? Even when we do have lapses, the force of nature brings our attention back to key things in our life in some way or another with a thought, a new friendship, new event or activity. We are not that far off we just play like we are when we need some reminding. Great news, with a BENEFICENT LIFE RECIPE, there is no need for any outside ingredients. Our inside ingredients will do just fine. You're already in receipt of all you need without realizing.

Let's start where it's relatable, remember when you were in school, and every year you graduated to another grade usually higher than the last. Some of you may have repeated, but you also advanced because you had experienced it before. You were a step ahead whether you thought you were or not. Now from that viewpoint, you were a star, even if you didn't know it! (Smile). There is always an opportunity to shine, no matter the situation, and since I come from that perspective; I believe I have the constant opportunity to bring life to every experience I encounter. I never take this opportunity for granted, and so I appreciate each and every opportunity I am given. Thank you, Divinity!

Each moment of our lives we have the opportunity to align with our place in conjunction with where our being is resonating at its particular time and place. We must attune to the conscious awareness of that beingness as it moves and develops to its deeper space. Our natural state of being yearns for its next life lesson which is one of life's purposes on this planet. When we stop achieving in this natural flow of life something starts dying off in us and we hinder life's progression. We can also add to the advancement of things just as well; we do have some part of that responsibility.

We all have gifts and purpose, and as long as we continue to be here, our journey still yearns for our active participation in this thing called life. Life needs our full attention and in that full attention is where LIFE'S RECIPE takes place. It is your guide to fulfillment and for the course completion. However, we have many ripples as we are living it, with questions such as the following. What do I do next? What happens from here? How do I get the results I am trying to achieve? If I had a sign – what do I need to change? I want to move forward to do what serves me, but I don't have a clue how to get there. What do I do now?

There are certain lines and statements that always stick to me, and in particular, this one does: If you want to get in touch with your life, look what is going on on the outside. This concept may give you a clear vision of what needs attending to. Our life happenings are the indicator. When it's time to lift up (which is an ongoing process in one's life), an indicator always comes along with a key message and a "push button" alert. This "push button" alert tries to get our attention in a multitude of ways, and when one becomes aware of this, we can adjust to life's plan and follow in accordance.

LIFE'S RECIPE is a mixture of your ingredients. At every level of uprise, there are outer circumstances that occur. These circumstances have energy and are in constant motion even when they are on pause they are still twirling around in the space like in orbit. When you have the recipe, you will be at a place where you can ride the winds in your sail, making life's adjustments to stay on course through the heaviest storms.

LIFE'S RECIPE INGREDIENTS

1. Overloaded and Overwhelmed (Alert Signal)

When these ingredients start churning, it means our life is in "out-of-balance" mode. While trying to stay in a place of balance, we get rid of old ingredients while stirring in new ones. This is good and means we are ready to move up a notch to our next development stage and is life's way of giving us a push toward achievement.

2. Rewind

To find stillness, watch the videotape of yourself through the day and make a list of everything you have done that doesn't seem to smoothly fit in.

3. Sensing

To find relaxation, look through your "rewind" list and notice your feelings. Is there excitement in your day? If there is no excitement, stop, look and listen.

4. Visualize

Observe your day. How do you want your day? Don't edit, judge or doubt. When a feeling sparks like a recharge moment, grab it and instantly write it down exactly as you experienced it.

5. Placement

Breathe and find order. Begin to orchestrate where the order can fit only by what feels comfortable and comforting enough to insert. At this point, it doesn't matter how much you put in place; it only matters that you start some placement.

6. Action

Start to be an active participant in your new role, find every opportunity to enhance this coming into being. When you start being in action, all pieces will start to follow your lead like a magnet. Be very conscious of this because your attraction is unleashed at this point. All the ingredients beforehand set the stage for this one in particular.

The six ingredients are necessary and vital to each part of the Beneficent Life Recipe; we are the hand mixer for each piece, and our involvement is where the wheel turns. Some of us have put our life on automatic, and in that process, our results have stayed the same when our inner state of being is pushing us toward a continuous growth ladder. While these two sides struggle against the other, neither side is winning. Both of those sides have been in the winner's circle, and both sides were workable at each stage. The only confusion is when one side outgrows the other, and we still hold on to the outgrown piece. As long as we live in the outgrown piece havoc takes over.

There is no need to live in havoc because it wrecks everything in sight, and we lose our true vision for ourselves. Unfortunately, we ignore the signal, and we think we must stay in this havoc. We had signs along the way, and we ignored them every time they flagged us. Our ingredients were mixing, and we were mixing with the mix-matched ingredients.

The Beneficent Life Recipe is a way to listen and take a new course of action. These six ingredients are useful throughout one's lifetime and offer continuous growth as part of a person's natural dynamic. There is no need to ask what's going on in our life because we can view our outer world to understand what's going on. If we are not in synch with what we see, we have the right to start mixing the ingredients and take charge from there. Now we have it our fingertips, and once we start to mix it up, we can rise upward and onward.

Beneficent life recipe is an uplifting, natural way of life to help us grow, evolve and develop. As we mix the ingredients, we gain a sense of freedom and power to support our livelihood and to live daily in the rhythm of our individual lives. If we feel out of place, disconnected, misaligned, unsatisfied then we are not in balance; we are disconnected from our navigator, and this navigator is our guiding light to life. What if I tell you this guiding light is self-assured and is the key to living up to your fullest potential? It is the vital, assured, highly valuable piece of information that's now ready to be implemented. Give yourself a new recipe in your life so you can release and soar to places you never knew you would come upon. Let yourself soar to the highest heights and enjoy your journey as you connect with your BENEFICENT LIFE RECIPE!

About Wanda Harris

Wanda Harris is a healer, teacher, and friend. She is a guided, gifted and intuitive individual who has spent the last two decades as a certified facilitator of the NAMELESS TECHNIQUE (a method of mental/physical releasing).

The NAMELESS TECHNIQUE is a unique approach for individuals who use verbal and written interactive exercises to aid in releasing behavioral patterns that cause mental and physical stresses.

The NAMELESS TECHNIQUE develops a heightened inner awareness that aligns one with personal growth goals. Her dynamism, humor, compassion, and love creates an uplifted and positive environment for her clients to grow and heal.

Wanda also lectures seminars and institutes ideas and programs targeted as "pioneers for a stress-free society."

Wanda Harris has an ongoing private practice in New Jersey.

To learn more about the NAMELESS TECHNIQUE or discovering your INNER BLUEPRINT,

Contact Wanda Today!

Website: http://stressfreesociety.net

Email: personalitymirroring@yahoo.com.

Final Thoughts

Outstanding Results is hard work. It takes a great coach along with great advice to work through the obstacles that may be standing in your way. If you want to achieve more, it takes the time and effort on your and your team's part to make it happen.

The authors in this book have shown you the proven track to obtain successful results in both business and life. What you do with this knowledge is up to you.

However, I know if may be difficult for you to get results. How do I know that? I know because before my clients come to work with me, they too were wishing to get results but they weren't getting the results they really wanted. Here is the key. The key is to stop wishing and start working.

So maybe you are facing the challenge of just getting started. You know you need to get started and you can't so you stopped. Another challenge you may be facing is you have tried something from this book, and it didn't work the way you expected, so you stopped. Here is another challenge, you chose something to work on from this book, and then you got distracted or worst stuck and you stopped. There seems to be a theme.

The theme is that you stopped. When you are working towards Outstanding Results, you can't stop. Think about climbing Mount Everest. There are people who want to and never get started, so they stop. There are those who try, and it didn't work out the way the wanted to so they stopped. There are those that start and get distracted or worst stuck. That is when disaster happens. It is only those climbers who don't stop and know when to ask for help who summit the mountain. These climbers know what it means to get results. Don't believe me? Go to Snapchat. There are two climbers who are broadcasting their whole adventure. It is very inspiring to those of us who want to get results.

The authors in this book are here to help you. So when you stop, I would urge you to reach out to that specific author and get their help. Go to their website, send them an email or simply call them. Do not accept being stopped. Once you do, you will not achieve the breakthrough results you want. We are all here to help you so don't be a stranger. We all look forward to helping you achieve the Outstanding RESULTS you want and deserve!

Jean Oursler

The Results Queen™

Notes

www.ingramcontent.com/pod-product-compliance
Lightning Source LLC
Chambersburg PA
CBHW071956090426
42740CB00011B/1959